Wokini

Other Hay House Titles of Related Interest

AMERICAN INDIAN PROPHECIES: Conversations with Chasing Deer,
by Kurt Kaltreider, Ph.D.

FROM THE HEART OF A GENTLE BROTHER, by Bartholomew

INFINITE SELF: 33 Steps to Reclaiming Your Inner Power, by Stuart Wilde

THE JOURNEY HOME: A Kryon Parable, by Lee Carroll

THE LOVE AND POWER JOURNAL: A Workbook for
the Fine Art of Living, by Lynn V. Andrews

PRACTICAL SPIRITUALITY, by John Randolph Price

All of the above titles are available through your local bookstore,
or may be ordered by calling Hay House at (800) 654-5126.

Please visit the Hay House Website at **www.hayhouse.com**

Mills Triumphs!... Praise for *Wokini*

"Billy Mills has . . . a winner . . . overwhelming and insightful."
— Peter Ueberroth, director, 1984 Olympics

"In Wokini *. . . Billy offers a powerful picture of the meaning of life. . . .
It will have a great impact on all Americans."*
— Al Neuharth, founder, *USA Today*

*"The reflections he writes about are wonderful. His values, knowledge, and dreams are
enlightening to anyone and well worth reading."*
— Pat Hingle, actor

"His message is one that will benefit anyone who listens."
— George Young, four-time Olympian

*"Billy tells us a story . . . about the important lessons of physical, emotional, and
spiritual strength. . . . It is from the heart, beautiful, filled with wisdom and truth."*
—York Onnen, director of program development,
President's Council, Physical Fitness and Sports

"Billy is an inspiration. . . . In Wokini, *he shares his insights on life that
make him so successful and a role model for all people."*
— John Echohawk, executive director, Native American Rights Fund

Wokini

A Lakota Journey to Happiness and Self-Understanding

Billy Mills

with Nicholas Sparks

Hay House, Inc., Carlsbad, CA

Published and distributed in the United States by:
Hay House, Inc., P.O. Box 5100, Carlsbad, CA 92018-5100
(800) 654-5126 • (800) 650-5115 (fax)

Editorial Supervision: Jill Kramer • *Design:* Jenny Richards
Illustrations: Jennifer Harper

Originally published in 1990 by Orion Books, a division of Crown Publishers

Library of Congress Cataloging-in-Publication Data

Mills, Billy.
    Wokini : a Lakota journey to happiness and self-understanding / Billy Mills with Nicholas Sparks.
        p.   cm.
    ISBN 1-56170-660-4 (pbk.)
    1. Happiness.   2. Teton philosophy—Miscellanea.   I. Sparks, Nicholas.   II. Title.
BJ1481.M64   1999
131—dc21
                                  99-22585
                                  CIP

ISBN 1-56170-660-4

02 01 00 99   4 3 2 1
First Printing, Hay House edition, July 1999

Printed in Canada

To Jill Sparks.
Her smile always filled my heart with joy.

❧ Acknowledgments ❧

Over the years, I have had the opportunity to know and love many people. Together, we've shared our lives, good times and bad. I would like to take this opportunity to thank a number of people who mean very much to me.

To Patricia
My friend, my companion,
my lover and my wife.

To my daughters and grandchildren
I hope all their wishes come true.

To my brothers and sisters
Who were always there
when I needed them.

To my father
Whose spirit still guides me.

To the Lakota Elders
Who helped me understand
the spirituality in my life.

To Nick and Cathy
My co-writer and his wife.
We are friends forever.

To all of you.
I hope this book helps you
come to know yourselves.

— Billy Mills

✑ Preface ✑

*W*okini, translated from Lakota, means "new life, a life of peace and happiness." This book teaches you about yourself, shows you what it means to be happy, and leads you on your own personal journey to feel more satisfied in your life. This book blends traditional Native American beliefs (which rely on meditation, thoughts, dreams, and love of nature's beauty) with modern therapeutic principles (positive thinking and an understanding of happiness), and is already helping hundreds of thousands of people across the country.

Wokini: Your Personal Journey to Happiness and Self-Understanding is an easily read allegory that shows you practical steps for improving every aspect of your life. As the story unfolds, you'll discover the myths associated with happiness, and learn the meaning of happiness and why it's important to be happy. Once you understand yourself, the book shows you a simple method to be happy whenever you want to be. It teaches you a powerful form of traditional meditation and guides you through ten outlooks that will make you a wiser, better, more loving person. By the book's conclusion, you will have learned a little bit about the Native American way of life, you will have come to understand yourself better, and you'll know some secrets about improving your life.

The book is short, simple, and easy to read. Most important, it works. If you do what this book teaches you, you'll find that you'll view the world in a more appreciative way, you'll know what it takes to make your dreams come true, and you'll make others wonder how you've done it. *Wokini* is a treasure—invaluable, irreplaceable, and priceless. Share its riches with yourself and others.

∞ Glossary ∞

Anpa wi   Sun

Ate   Father

Cantesica   Despair, sadness

Iktumi   Spider; in this book, the trickster spider, based upon Lakota legend

Mnihuha   Cloth

Paha Sapa   The Black Hills of South Dakota. The heart of everything that is. It is a very holy place in Lakota Sioux culture.

Sota   Smoke

Tiwahe   Family

Tunkasila The presence of God through wisdom. The wise grandfather of all living things.

Wakantanka God. The Father in the Sky. The Creator of the world.

Wicahpis Stars

Wokahnigapi Oiglake Journey of understanding (actually, understanding journey).

Wokini New life. Happiness.

These words are translated from Lakota to English. Some have been spelled phonetically to aid the reader in pronunciation due to the difficulty of the Lakota language.

WOKINI

✆ The Scroll ✆

A Lesson in Happiness

HAPPINESS IS A WONDERFUL FEELING. IT MAKES YOU FEEL GOOD IN ANY SIT-
UATION. IT GIVES YOU HOPE IN TIMES OF DESPAIR. IT MAKES YOU FEEL PEACE
IN A WORLD OF TURMOIL. I WANT YOU TO BE HAPPY ANYTIME YOU WISH IT.
TO DO THAT, YOU ARE INVITED TO TRAVEL AND LEARN WITH DAVID, A YOUNG
INDIAN WHO LEARNED THE SECRET OF BEING HAPPY.

Two things happened that year that affected the rest of David's life. The first thing brought sadness to him. The second taught him the greatest secret he had ever learned. Either way, he wouldn't forget that miraculous summer in South Dakota nearly thirty years ago.

It had been one of the hottest summers in recent memory. The crops had withered from the drought, and fourteen more cows had been found dead in Henry Bear Claw's pasture three days ago. The weakest were the first to die, starting with the old, the young, and the diseased. It was the way of *Wakantanka,* and it helped keep nature in balance. The strong lived and would breed strong offspring. It was the way of the world, the way it had always been and always would be. Henry, though, didn't see it that way. He had never been able to look past his pocketbook.

Food was scarce, and the little water that remained in the wells was polluted from the mining activity of twenty years ago. People were afraid this summer would end their way of life. But that's not why David was afraid. They would get by, he knew; they always did. The Lakota had survived wars, natural disasters, and smallpox. A drought wouldn't kill them. But David was still afraid, more afraid than he had ever been.

His father hadn't come to church this morning.

The spiritual ramifications didn't frighten him nearly as much as the possible reason why his father stayed home. Something bad must have happened.

He was right.

This was the first thing that affected the rest of his life.

David could see the billowing *sota* in the distance as he returned home. He suddenly felt sick. *She had died,* he thought to himself, *and my father is burning her bed so we don't get sick, too.* He wanted to cry but didn't because he didn't want to upset any of his younger brothers and sisters. *I have to be a man,* he thought to himself, although he was still only a young boy. *My family needs me to be strong.*

David's siblings were not all of the same blood. Actually, most of them were half brothers, half sisters, step siblings, and adopted members of the family. Even if you had little room in your house, it was the duty of the Indians to help their family—not simply family in a typical, nuclear sense, but family in the broader sense that all living creatures are connected and related. It didn't seem strange to David to believe in such things as the circle of creation in which everything is connected. It was his way, just as it was his father's way, and his father's.

His sister was buried three days later at the edge of the cemetery just inside the entrance. The plot didn't have any trees near it, and the sun was going to make the weeds grow very fast. David would try to keep them under control, but he knew it would be difficult. School and chores took up much of his time. Still, the fact that weeds would grow on her grave didn't bother him nearly as much as the location of the plot; it was only a couple of feet from the entrance road of the cemetery. People would trample on it as they walked through the cemetery. And worse, the road would be widened one day, probably within the next few years, and his sister would find her body being moved to a more convenient place so the Buicks and Pontiacs could roll through to allow the more privileged to visit their loved ones.

It reminded him of his ancestors being taken from their burial mounds and moved to the attic of the Smithsonian so the intellectuals could poke and prod their remains only to find out that they were just the same as you and me. Indians had never been treated with respect. Still, this plot was better than none, and besides, it was all they could afford. His father had sold the car to pay for the expenses of the funeral. David couldn't understand why bad things always seemed to happen to his family. He didn't want to be told again that life on the reservation was never easy. Simple answers like that were given by people who had lost hope. David didn't like such people.

David had loved his sister deeply, as he had loved his mother, who had died three years earlier when he was eleven. That year was very hard for him. He expected this year to be no different. Pain, sadness, loneliness, and empty memories were all he had to show for their deaths.

Then depression set in. With it came the fear that David was losing control. The feeling was so powerful, it was like standing in the river with the strong current flowing around his body. It pushed him, made him weak, and in time would win. That kind of power always won.

David missed his sister terribly. He missed her because she was his sister *and* his best friend. He missed her because he loved the things she did and said. And . . . without his sister, the days would seem longer, deeper, and darker than ever. David felt a special kinship with her. She had helped raise the younger children in the family after his mother had died, and David believed that she had been responsible for keeping the family together. It had been a very hard time for everyone, yet her strength during this horrible period had lifted David's heart many times. She was his counselor and friend. She studied with him and taught him math in a way that his teacher never could. She played games with him, walked and fished with him, and told stories to him every night. And now . . . she was gone. Gone forever . . . and David would never see her again. The thought of that made David cry for hours on end. He would sit by the river and stare aimlessly at the flowing water. There were many times when he considered jumping in just to end it all. Little did he know, his was the most powerful and destructive form of depression. It kept him awake at night, it ate away at his heart and soul, and would eventually lead him to the Land of Darkness.

Luckily, David wasn't the type to kill himself. He was too young to give up hope. Even if he wanted to, he didn't know if he had the courage. There was, however, an even more important reason he wouldn't take his own life. *It was something his sister wouldn't understand.* True, he knew she was dead, yet . . . there were times when he felt her within him, alive and powerful. He didn't know if he was imagining it, but he heeded it nonetheless—the feeling was simply too powerful to ignore.

In the early mornings and late afternoons, David could almost hear his sister talking to him; her laughter mingled with the sounds of chirping birds, and her whispers floated with the wind. He felt from his heart that she was trying to communicate with him. David thought for many days as to her reason for this, but his depression clouded his thoughts. In all, it took almost two weeks for him to realize that what she really wanted for him was to be happy again.

Happiness.

David wanted to be happy again. He longed for the feeling of peace and contentment in his life. His sister had been able to overcome her grief when their mother had died. Could he not do it, too?

He didn't know.

David wished for the strength his sister had many years ago. He knew he couldn't expect to suddenly forget everything that had happened to him. That would always stay with him. Yet, where would he find the strength he needed? And most important, how could he be happy again?

The question awakened him in the morning, it followed him through school and his daily chores, and it was the last thing he thought of before sleeping.

How could he be happy again? That's what he wanted to know. The answer would be worth all the priceless gems in the world. If he had a way to be happy again, he would know the meaning of life itself. And most important, he would be able to do what his sister wished. But . . . could he find the answer himself? He considered himself to be smart, but not nearly as smart as that. No, he knew, the answer would have to come from somewhere else.

Or from someone else.

But who would know such an answer? *Perhaps I should talk to my* "ate." (David always called his father *ate*—pronounced "ah-Tay"—the Lakota word for "father.") *He will know what to do.*

Like all young boys, David regarded his *ate* as a very special man. He seemed to tower above David, his shoulders strong from a lifetime of labor. His *ate* was a man who held his head high, a man who respected himself and all living creatures. There was grace in the way he moved, a silent strength that David longed to understand. *Where* did he learn it? His *ate* had no formal education, he had never studied with the tribal elders, and had not learned to read until past the age of twenty. Was his father telling the truth when he said that he learned all he knew from the twinkling stars and the melting rays of the sun? Or did he find peace of heart and soul in the tree grove where he often sat alone with his thoughts? Did he really hear his forefathers' souls in the winds of the plains? David didn't know.

Yet there was something besides knowledge that made David feel awe when he was near his *ate*. Put simply, David's father was happy, and it was a kind of happiness David had never known. It was a spiritual self-understanding and acceptance, an internal love that radiated from him every minute of his life. It didn't matter if things went well for him. Nor did it depend on how others treated him. It was as if there was nothing that could get him down.

His father also had a way of looking at the world and appreciating the little things. He would smile when he heard the birds sing early in the morning; he would laugh at the problems that confronted him. He loved life, as all people should, and enjoyed it to the fullest. David longed to be like him.

David waited until nightfall to speak with his *ate*. They were sitting in the main room—the other two rooms were used as bedrooms for his family. It was a clean room, although a bit cluttered, but fifteen people in a two-bedroom house makes it nearly impossible to keep tidy at all times. It would never be shown in *Better Homes and Gardens,* but it was his home and he was proud of it. The only lamp in the room sat behind the radio, which softly played Tommy Dorsey in the background. His father sat in the easy chair and was looking over the *Reader's Digest.* His younger brothers and sisters were in bed, and his older siblings had stepped out for a moment.

In a low voice, David whispered, "*Ate,* I want to be happy again, and I want you to help me. I'm very depressed about Emma's death. I've been losing sleep, and I can't seem to concentrate anymore."

The father eyed David intently for a moment before nodding his head in understanding. He smiled, turning up the corners of his mouth slightly. *He has grown so quickly,* the father thought to himself. *The time has come for him to learn.*

The father set the magazine down on the end table and rose from his chair. He walked to an old battered desk that sat in the corner. His back ached from the day's work, but he knew the pain was nothing when compared with what he would give his son. He opened a drawer, rummaged through it for a moment, and pulled out a worn piece of *mnihuha,* carefully rolled as a scroll. David knew a little about the scroll although he had never been allowed, or so he thought, to study it. Rooted in Indian tradition, the scroll was hand-painted by his great-great-grandfather, a medicine man. It detailed *Wokahnigapi Oiglake,* a journey of understanding.

The father handed the scroll to David.

"Take this and you'll learn," the father said.

David took it and carefully unrolled it. What he saw surprised him.

The scroll contained a series of seven pictures, some more elaborate than others. No words were printed beneath them. David looked to his *ate.* He wasn't sure what to do with it.

"I don't understand what it means."

The father smiled and shook his head. He turned from his son and smiled as he looked out the window. The sky was growing dark, and *wicahpis* began to twinkle. The *wicahpis,* appearing slowly as if by magic, had always captivated him.

Finally, he answered in a low voice. "It shows you how to be happy in your life. That's what you wanted me to tell you, isn't it?"

David nodded. "Uh-huh. I don't know what these pictures mean, though. How can it help me if I don't know what they mean?"

"My son, you must learn what they mean."

David knew the answer to the next question even before his *ate* answered. "Are you going to tell me?"

"No, I think it's best if you find the meaning yourself. Words can only teach you a little of what you must know. You will learn more quickly if you use the scroll to guide you."

David rubbed his jaw reflectively. "Guide me? Guide me to where?"

"Take it with you on your journey."

David looked up with surprise. "A journey? Where am I supposed to go?"

The father turned around and faced his son. He took hold of his son's shoulder. "There's no set path to follow. It's a journey of understanding. You should do what you think is best to find the meaning of the pictures."

"Who would be able to tell me the meanings?"

"Someone wiser than me. Someone who can reach your inner soul and communicate with you. Someone you trust and admire."

The father knew he wasn't telling his son everything he could, but he had a reason. The journey was an experience, not a lesson. David, on the other hand, was disturbed. He couldn't understand his *ate's* reluctance to tell him what he wanted to know.

"When am I to leave?" David asked.

"The sooner you begin your journey, the sooner you'll understand everything you need to know." His *ate* returned his gaze to the *wicahpis.*

David left his *ate* after it became clear that he would learn no more from him. He took the scroll to his room and studied it for hours before he finally went to sleep. Although his school educated him in the ways of the *Wasicu*, he had learned much of Indian lore on his own. Surely it would help him.

He did not sleep very well that night.

The next morning, just as the *anpa wi* was rising, David ate a large breakfast. He decided to travel with only a small knapsack in which he carried the scroll. He saw no need to take anything else with him—he didn't think he'd be gone that long. After saying good-bye to his *tiwahe,* he left the house and walked up the dirt road that led to the edge of the reservation. His *Wokahnigapi Oiglake* had begun.

David thought he should first go to see Ben Long Feather. The thought had come to him while dressing. It was as if *Wakantanka* had personally placed that idea in his mind. Ben Long Feather worked in the Indian museum at the edge of the reservation. Surely he could tell him more about the meaning of the scroll. He was, after all, one of the wisest Indians on the reservation.

A few hours later, David arrived at the museum. When he walked in, he asked a young receptionist named Mary if he could speak to Ben Long Feather. The receptionist looked him over very carefully. She saw sadness in the young boy's eyes. There was no mistaking that he was in pain. She could see the hurt in the way he looked and moved. After a moment, she left her desk and walked to a small room.

David took the scroll from his knapsack while he waited and studied it for a little while longer. A couple of things were familiar. The first picture was *Iktumi,* the trickster spider, about to be eaten by an eagle. But how could *Iktumi* relate to happiness? Could it make him happy again? And most important, how long was it going to take for him to be happy again?

After a few minutes, Ben Long Feather approached him. Ben was seventy-nine years old (David knew that from school) but looked to be no older than fifty. Few wrinkles, only light traces of gray on the sides of his head—that was all there was. *He couldn't be that old,* David thought to himself.

Ben walked up to him and shook David's hand. "You wanted to see me?"

"Yes," David answered.

"Come with me."

Ben led David to his office. As they walked, David saw a peaceful contentment on Ben's face that reminded him of his father. *Ben knew the answer, too,* David thought to himself as Ben pushed the door open. *Ben knew how to be happy.* David hoped Ben would share it with him.

The office was cluttered with Indian items, carefully tagged, but not yet on display. It was plain to see that Ben loved his work very much. David took the scroll from his knapsack and handed it to him.

Ben Long Feather looked at the scroll for a moment. He asked, "How can I help you?"

"I don't know what it means. I'd like you to tell me."

"I see," Ben said as he nodded, a slight smile on his face. He took a few moments before speaking. He seemed to be looking for the right words. Finally, he said, "The *mnihuha* has been stretched and dried. It's very old. I would think one of your own ancestors made it. The pictures themselves are hand-painted, using natural clays and oils. I've seen these types of scrolls before. They are used as a tool for teaching Indians anything they want to know. The pictures are symbolic of a journey. Taken as a whole, the scroll details the legend of a young Indian's journey to understanding. It's called *Wokahnigapi Oiglake.*"

David knew that Ben was hiding the truth from him just as his *ate* had done.

"My *ate* said it would be able to make me happy."

Ben smiled and nodded his head. "Your *ate* is a very wise man."

"I need to know what the pictures mean. Can you tell me?"

"No, I'm sorry. I'm not qualified to tell you. You must meet someone with more experience than I have—someone who can communicate with your inner self. Only that person can tell you what it means."

The same answer his father had given him, David thought. It was an answer that didn't help him. David felt the tears begin to well in his eyes again. *Why wouldn't anyone help him? Why wouldn't anyone tell him what the scroll meant?*

David's face reddened, and his voice cracked as he asked, "Who can tell me?"

Ben was silent and looked at him with a calm, peaceful smile. David returned his gaze, his own expression distressed and ridden with anxiety.

"Bend near me, David," Ben whispered in the young Indian's ear. "Closer still. I have something to give to you."

At that moment, Ben Long Feather took David by the arm. As he did, something wonderful happened. David no longer saw the gentle face of Ben Long Feather. Instead, he saw other faces, thousands of them appearing and disappearing. There was the face of his grandfather, his mother, and his sister, all intermingled, yet each distinct. He saw animals, hundreds of different kinds, and he saw the land where he lived. Places came and went as if they were being driven by a tornado. David then felt himself become part of the tornado. He rose high, and his world began to spin. The pit of his stomach rose and fell. Suddenly, thousands of thoughts came rushing to him, most of them too fast to understand. Thoughts of life, love, dreams, pictures, people, and animals spread through his mind with an intensity he had never before experienced. The rush of thoughts filled his mind to its capacity, and when he thought it would burst . . .

The thoughts stopped and all was still. Darkness enveloped him. David didn't know where he was or what he was doing. The darkness brought fear to him. As his vision persisted, his sister appeared far in the distance. At first, she was no more than a pinpoint of light. Gradually, she came closer to him. She was facing him and she glowed. It was a deep white glow that seemed not dangerous but powerful. David felt her living again, she was breathing, her heart was beating. And she was talking to David. David couldn't hear her, but he felt her words inside him. *She was telling him to go on, telling him not to give up.* He would find the knowledge he was looking for if he simply persisted. And then she was gone.

David's world came back to him with the same rush of intensity that he had felt moments before. David felt as if he would faint as soon as his vision had faded. David closed his eyes, caught his balance, and listened to Ben's answer. Ben answered David's earlier question as though nothing out of the ordinary had transpired. Had any of this really happened, or was it a dream?

"This person is for you to find on your own. I can't help you." Ben handed the scroll back to David. "Good luck, young man. I admire you for undertaking the journey. I remember mine very well. You'll learn a lot. You'll learn the secret of life itself."

David left the museum more depressed than ever. He had felt his sister; he knew she was watching over him, but still he felt horrible. He was breathing too quickly, he had knots in his stomach, and his legs shook as he walked. He felt as if he were losing control. The thoughts of his vision came back to him, lingered with him, and made him feel weak and dizzy. David staggered to a tree and sat beneath it. As he put his face in his hands to try to regain control of himself, the tears burst forth. He cried for what seemed like hours. His body shook, and his heart felt a sadness that he had never experienced. He felt utterly alone.

Once his emotions had been spent, he felt tired but more in control. He wiped the tears, sniffled, and began to take deep breaths. After a few minutes, he was able to think about what had happened in the museum. Now, he wasn't sure if his vision had been real or imaginary. It seemed real, but the more he thought about it, the more it slipped from his mind. The vision became clouded, almost muddy. *It must have been a dream,* he finally concluded.

Yet deep in his heart, David knew it wasn't a dream. Although the details were forgotten, the purpose of his sister's visit stayed with him. The vision had become part of him and had shown him where to go. He now knew the person who could communicate with his soul.

Tunkasila Paha Sapa. The Man in the Hills. The wise Grandfather of all living things.

David set out for *Paha Sapa*, the Black Hills of South Dakota. *Paha Sapa* holds a special place in Indian religion and legend. It is a holy place, defined literally as *the heart of everything that is.*

The thought of knowing where he was going helped him forget his sadness

18

for just a short while. He thought instead of the journey to *Paha Sapa*. It was a two-day walk to *Paha Sapa*—David had traveled there many times—and since he had no money, he had no choice but to walk. He had no food, but didn't worry. He knew how to fish and eat off the land—that is, if he felt like eating. His appetite had been practically nonexistent since his sister's death.

The two days of contemplation and the journey weren't able to help David. After the first few hours, David's thoughts returned to loneliness. The lack of food and strain on his body had made him weak and vulnerable to the feelings of depression. Soon he no longer cared about the journey itself—his grief took hold of him, strangling him with despair. For two days, David moved like a starving wolf, without thought and without care.

David arrived at *Paha Sapa* early in the afternoon. He had learned from Indian lore that the Man lived in a cabin, about a mile south of the River Bend and near the Indian Needle—a large pointed rock high in the hills. He was able to find his way easily, although the climb itself was difficult. When he reached the top of the mountain, he was somewhat surprised that the Indian legend was true. The cabin was there, just like the legends said it would be, and sitting outside was an old man. The Man seemed to be waiting for him, as if he knew David was coming to visit him. The Man motioned for David to come toward him, and David did.

The Man poured him a cup of tea. He smiled as he handed it to David.

"You must be thirsty. The climb is very hard."

David took the cup and drank from it. The tea soothed his parched throat. The Man said, "I'm glad you have come, David."

David looked at him with wide eyes.

How does he know my name? David wondered. David felt frightened for just a moment. Sure, it was eerie, but there was something about the Man that made his comment seem natural, not strange. And David trusted him immediately. It wasn't the way he looked so much as the way he *was.* He was almost larger than life itself, and David knew the Man realized his place in the world was that of a teacher—a great and generous teacher who would give his wisdom to all who came to him.

The Man stood and walked into his house, leaving the door open for the young Indian to enter. David finished his tea and followed after.

The cabin seemed typical to David. It reminded him of his own home. It was cluttered with various items—faded photographs, an old radio, a table and chairs, and Indian artwork. *Just like anyone else,* David thought, and the Man looked at him. David felt suddenly, from the depths of his heart, that the

Man read this thought. David would have to be careful around him—his thoughts were his own, and no other person had the right to intrude upon them.

"I agree," the Man said softly, and David felt the Man leave his mind. David knew his thoughts were his own again, which made him feel more at ease.

The Man took a hand-stitched blanket from an old case that sat in the corner.

David asked, "How did you know my name?"

The Man in the Hills answered with a smile. "I've been expecting you."

"You have?" David asked curiously.

The Man in the Hills spread the blanket on the floor and sat. David sat across from him, then took the scroll from his knapsack.

"You've begun your journey," the Man in the Hills said as he made himself comfortable. "I'm very pleased. It makes me feel good that our ways are still being taught."

David looked at the scroll. "My *ate* gave me this, and I think you're the one who can tell me what it means."

"Something disturbs you, my young friend. What's bothering you?"

Perhaps it was the way the Man asked him, or perhaps it was simply the

Man's presence—David would never know—but what happened to him at that moment would never be forgotten. Unlike the vision he had with Ben, the vision inspired by the Man was more subtle—and yet far more powerful. It was as if David's soul floated from his body and soared over the plains, coasted with the wind, circled like the birds, and then shot straight up toward the stars. He felt free and loved—a vessel filled with understanding. He had never experienced such peace of heart and soul. He became one with nature, reveling in its beauty and absorbing all the lessons it could teach him. His purity of soul lightened his cares and worries. He felt one with *Wakantanka*. . . .

The vision faded suddenly just as it had done with Ben.

Just as quickly as the vision had come to him and his soul floated free, he felt his body and soul come together in this world. He no longer felt free, but felt burdened and heavy, like a rock unmoved throughout the centuries. In his heart, he felt the rock of sadness and depression. His heart filled with despair once again.

The sudden change in emotions shocked his system. He broke out in a cold sweat and had trouble catching his breath. Finally, he answered the Man's question.

"I've come to see you because I'm very sad. My sister passed away a short time ago. It hurts me very much—I loved her, and now I know I'll never see her again."

The Man nodded in understanding, a sympathetic look in his eyes.

David went on. "I mean, she's gone . . . gone forever. I just don't understand. She was young . . . she . . . she had her whole life in front of her. I miss her terribly."

David started to cry. He couldn't help it. The memory of his sister's death overwhelmed him. His soul ached, and his heart felt heavy.

The Man leaned forward and placed his hand on David's shoulder.

"Death is always hard to understand. But, my young friend, your sister has not left your life completely. She is with you now as she always will be. She feels your pain and is saddened by it. She wants nothing more than for you to be happy."

"How . . . how do you know?"

"*I know.* My young friend, you must separate your sister's physical life from her spiritual life. She's not gone forever—she's changed into something far greater than you or I. She is with the Great Spirit; she is sharing in His wonder. And most important, she's alive within you! *David, your sister will never leave you!* When you're confronted with a problem, you'll think of what she would have told you to do. She'll be with you always to help you when times become difficult. Her spirit is soaring—she is free and at peace. All her dreams have come true, and her wisdom will find its way into your life."

David listened but was still sad. He spoke softly. "But when I think about how . . . how she . . . she was such a wonderful person. It hurts me to know she's gone."

The Man's expression was sympathetic. He spoke slowly as he held David's shoulder. His touch was soothing, yet powerful. He knew the art of true communication.

"The pain you're feeling will go away in time and will be replaced with love and happy memories of your childhood with her. This is your sister's special gift to you. You can use your memories of your sister to keep her alive in this world *as long as you live*. It's up to you to teach others how special she was in your life. If you do so, they'll learn and come to know her as well as you knew her, and she'll live forever in both worlds."

David knew that mere words could not help him at this moment. Yet even at his young age, he also knew he should try to remember what the Man told him. He knew it would be important to help him come to terms with his loss.

"Are you sure?"

From the way the Man closed his eyes and nodded, David knew that the Man was speaking the truth. He had never seen a person so sure about anything, and it made him feel a bit better.

The Man answered, "Yes. *All life is connected.* You'll carry a piece of her the rest of your life. She is surviving in you, my friend."

They didn't speak for a few moments. David wiped the tears from his face. In time he said, "I've been depressed for many days now, and it's tearing my life apart."

"Is that why you've come to me? Do you want to know how to be happy again?"

"Uh-huh," David said as he nodded. The Man smiled broadly. His eyes glowed and twinkled. Smile lines had been etched in the Man's face, and David watched in wonder as the Man seemed to radiate his positive feelings from within him. His expression made David feel better.

David looked at the scroll still clutched in his hand and passed it to the Man.

"Can you tell me what the pictures mean? My *ate* said if I found their meanings, I would learn what I need to know. He said I would be happy again."

The Man spoke almost as if he was in awe of the power of happiness.

"I'm glad you desire happiness, my young friend. That's the first step in understanding this feeling and making it part of your life. Once you desire happiness, it will find you and will allow you to come to terms with your loss in a way that will make you feel good about your life. Happiness will allow you to feel hope in the darkest of situations and peace in a world of turmoil. Happiness will allow your dreams to come true! *It's the most beautiful feeling in the world, and it never has to leave your life!* To be happy, you simply need desire and the knowledge of how to be happy. The meanings of the pictures on the scroll will show you everything you need to know. They will make it very clear to you."

"Will you tell me?"

"I'll help you in every way I can. It's my deepest desire for you and everyone to be happy in life. But this is your journey—the pictures will mean slightly different things to different people, including you. The meaning of the scroll in your life is for you to discover."

"What do I have to do to learn?"

"You must leave here and find the meaning of the first picture."

David examined the first picture. It was an image of *Iktumi,* the trickster spider, about to be eaten by an eagle. He asked, "The picture of *Iktumi?*"

"Yes," the Man said.

"Should I learn the legend of *Iktumi?*"

"In a way. Don't ask people to explain the legend to you—that will do you no good. Ask eight people the question you are seeking to answer. The meaning of the picture will become clear after you find your answers."

"Which eight people?"

"Any eight. They will provide the meaning of the first picture. *You must ask them how to be happy.*"

The question struck David as odd. That was the reason he had come to *Paha Sapa.* And besides, how did happiness relate to *Iktumi?*

The Man went on. "It's important to find eight different answers from the people you ask. Return to me when you've completed the task. We'll then be able to explain the meaning of the first picture."

David sat quietly for a moment. His journey was going to take longer than he had thought. He had to meet and talk to people, but whom? Whom was he supposed to talk to?

"Do the people have to be Indians?"

"No. Their answers must be different. That's the only requirement."

"What if they can't tell me the right answers?"

"All answers will lead to understanding. Don't worry."

David did worry when he left, though. He didn't know where to start. For a moment, he wanted to return home.

The Man in the Hills spoke to him as he walked away. "Don't stop now—you will find the right answers. It's easier than you think."

David didn't return until three days had passed.

∞ The Lesson of *Iktumi* ∞
The Meaning of the First Picture

IKTUMI IS THE LAKOTA WORD FOR "SPIDER." IKTUMI IS REGARDED AS A TRICKSTER AND LIAR. IKTUMI CAN CAUSE A PERSON TO BELIEVE THINGS THAT AREN'T TRUE. HE IS VERY DANGEROUS BECAUSE OF THIS POWER. IKTUMI HAS THE ABILITY TO RUIN A PERSON'S LIFE.

The Man in the Hills smiled as David made his way up the mountain. David had a disturbed look on his face. He was still sad—his journey had not seemed to help.

"Have you found what you needed?" the Man in the Hills asked.

"I'm not sure. I asked everyone I met. Many of them had the same answers. None of them seemed to help me, though. I still don't feel much better."

"Have you found eight different ways to be happy?"

"Uh-huh. I wrote them down, but I don't understand any more than when I left."

"Yes, you do. You just don't realize it yet. Come in. Let us prepare."

The preparations were completed after an hour. A blanket was spread on the floor, twigs were set afire in a small urn, and the only lighting was provided by two torches, one behind each person. The shadows flickered. The Man sat quietly for a long while with his eyes closed. David watched him, wondering what he was doing. Finally, the Man opened his eyes and spoke.

"Tell me what you have learned."

"You mean tell you how to be happy?"

The Man smiled. "You can phrase it that way if you desire."

David thought for a second for the right place to start, and began. "When I left here, I went toward town. After an hour of walking around, I met someone who would answer the question. He was an older man who lived near town. He was very poor. The house he lived in was almost falling apart. He said that he couldn't afford to eat until he received his check from the government. When I asked him how to be happy, *he said that if he had more money, then he'd be happy.*"

"How did that answer strike you?"

David pondered the question for a while. He could not answer—something was holding him back. But what was it? What was preventing him from answering the question? Was it his mind or . . . or was it something else? He felt faint, as if he would pass out any second. The world spun, it twirled around him, and David grew slightly nauseated. Luckily, the truth came to him before he became ill. The truth was simple—and it had been told to him from someone beyond this world. It was clear that his sister was guiding him, leading him to the right answers. He could not see her, he could not hear her, but he knew she was there. He could feel her inside him, bringing the truth to his lips. He knew what she wanted him to say.

He said simply, "It bothered me."

The Man smiled again. "Good. You *have* learned. Tell me, why did it bother you?"

This time, David didn't have to pause before answering. He said quickly, "It didn't make sense to me. I'm sure he believed it, but money can't make you happy. You can use money for many things, but you can't use it to buy happiness."

The Man looked to the burning urn as he spoke. He had a peaceful expression on his face. "You're right, my young friend. The desire for wealth as a way to be happy is one I've heard often, *despite the fact it's untrue.* A person must realize it's their attitude that needs to be enriched, not their wallets. Money is only as important in life as a person makes it. A person can be happy without money if they want to be. *Happiness has no favorites*—but it can't be bought with wealth."

"I know," David said as he nodded. "Many poor people I met were as happy or happier than the rich people. In fact, I heard a story during my journeys about a rich man who had committed suicide. If a person only needed money to be happy, then explain to me why he killed himself."

The Man took a small jar that sat next to him and opened it. He took out a small pebble and placed it to the side. Then he answered, "It can't be explained, unless you learn and *believe that happiness doesn't depend on money—it depends on you and your attitude!* Now, what was the second answer you found?"

David answered quickly. "Fame. *I met a person who said that if he were famous, then he'd be happy.* You see, he wants to be a movie star."

"Ah, yes. Fame is very important to many people. Did that answer make sense to you?"

David shook his head. "No. That answer bothered me as much as the first."

"Why?"

"For the same reasons. Fame can't make a person happy—if it did, then all famous people would be happy. But many people are famous, yet not all are happy. The way I see it, fame has many responsibilities and some advantages, but it can't make you happy."

"You're right again," the Man answered. *"Happiness comes from within a person, not from what they do or who they are.* You must learn and believe that you can be happy whether or not you're famous. Happiness is available to all. It doesn't depend on how many people know you! It's not the panacea you're looking for if you want to be happy. If you're happy, you don't need fame. If you're famous, happiness comes from within you, not from the fame."

The Man took another pebble from the jar and placed it next to the first. "Now, what was the third answer you found?"

"Well, later that day, I talked to a young woman who lives alone in town. I asked her if money and fame would make her happy, and she answered no. Money and fame don't mean anything to her—she has nearly everything she wants. Yet, she was rather depressed despite all the good things in her life, and she said she'd never be happy until she got the one thing she wanted. *She said that if she could find the right person to marry, then she'd be happy."*

"Do you believe she was right?"

"No. I don't think so. Having the right spouse is very important, but I don't think it can make you happy all the time. I've met people—I even met one on my journey—who loved their spouses, but it wasn't enough to make them happy."

The Man took another pebble from the jar and placed it to the side as he spoke. "To say that another person can make you happy is to do yourself a great injustice. It's the same as saying someone else has control of your emotions. But anyone who is in touch with their soul knows it isn't true. The feeling of happiness comes from within *you,* not from somewhere else. It's up to you, and only you, to control how you feel."

David nodded in understanding. The Man said, "Tell me about the person with a good marriage you said you met on your journey. You said she was unhappy?"

"Well, like I said, she told me she loved her husband. He's the most perfect man she could ever dream of. But she didn't feel good about her life, so I asked her what it meant to be happy."

"And she said?"

"She said that she would be happy if she had more friends. She had dreamed of being popular ever since she was a young child, and she didn't have many friends of her own. She said she was rather lonely, despite her good marriage."

The Man placed the fourth pebble to the side. "Having friends has nothing to do with being happy except for the fact that if you're happy, you'll have more friends. It's like the other things people believe are necessary for happiness—these are things that deny its very beauty. People assume they must have something before they can be happy, as if happiness must be earned or deserved. Nothing could be further from the truth. In the end, you must realize that you can be happy even if you have no friends at all, and that having friends cannot guarantee happiness."

David agreed quickly. "I learned from the next person I met that having a lot of friends doesn't guarantee happiness. This woman was very popular with everyone. She had more friends than anyone I met on my journey."

"And she was happy?"

"No, not really. She was nice and kind. She even invited me into her house for dinner. I could see why she was so popular—she seemed to like everyone as much as they liked her. All the neighborhood children called her 'Auntie,' and she had invitations to dozens of parties. She was more popular than anyone I've ever met. But when I asked her if she was happy, she said no."

"Why did she say no?"

"Well, you'd have to meet her. You see, she's very heavy, and her face is scarred from a childhood bout with chicken pox. *She said that she'd be happy if she were attractive.* She said she cries about it when she's alone. I tried to tell her that looks don't mean as much as kindness to others, but I couldn't convince her—she wouldn't listen to me."

The Man felt bad for the woman. He placed the fifth pebble to the side. "It's a very sad thing when people can't accept who they are. It is even worse when they believe they have to change something before they can be happy. Beauty cannot make a person happy—even beautiful people must learn to be happy. And if you want to be happy, you can be—you won't be excluded because of the way you look."

Slowly but surely, David thought he was beginning to understand how happiness related to *Iktumi*, the trickster spider. He didn't understand everything yet, but he knew he would in a short while.

"What did you do after you left her?"

"Well, it was getting late, so I found a barn to sleep in. I found another man there. It was very sad. He was blind, and his leg had been amputated in

World War II. He was living as a beggar in the streets and was very unhappy with his life. *He said that if he wasn't physically disabled, then he'd be happy."*

The Man had heard this many times. He placed the sixth pebble to the side.

"Physical health is one of the things so many people take for granted. The simple pleasures of walking in the sunshine, listening to the roar of a river, or seeing the beauty of a sunset are experiences that many can only dream of. All able people should focus on what they have and take the time to enjoy those simple pleasures. It would help a person appreciate how special life really is. Yet, these simple things have nothing to do with whether a person is happy or not. A physical disability need not ruin a person's life. Happiness isn't limited to those in perfect health. Despite all the physical limitations in the world, you can be happy if you want to be. I want you to realize that happiness is a feeling that comes from within you—and nothing that happens to you need affect it."

"I'm beginning to understand that now."

"You have also begun to understand the purpose of your journey, whether or not you realize it. Did you find your seventh answer the following day?"

"Uh-huh. I found a young woman who was selling her home. She said it had too many memories. Her husband had passed away. *She said she'd be happy if her spouse hadn't died."*

The Man looked toward the ground. He placed the seventh pebble to the side. "This is the same reason you have been unhappy. You must have known exactly how she felt."

"Yeah, I did. I tried to tell her the things you told me, but they didn't seem to help her."

The Man began in a low voice, "Death—it has been feared in our society since the dawn of man. Yet, it is not the end of life; it is the beginning of a new life. A person should take the time to realize that a person who dies is not gone; that person is changed into something far greater. And as I told you, memories can keep a person alive in this world far longer than you or I can ever hope to live. A person must begin to realize these things. In time, grief will be followed with any emotion you choose. And despite what you think, you can be happy again. Maybe not right away, but certainly with the passage of time. If you doubt what I have said, simply ask yourself a question: *Do you honestly believe that your deceased loved one wants you to be unhappy?* If the answer is no, then you must work to become happy to honor that person."

The two sat in silence for a moment. The Man took a small pot of tea and poured two cups. He handed one to the young man. "Tell me the final way to be happy."

"It took most of the day, but I finally found someone with a different reason. He said that he was worried about peace, he worried about the environment, he worried about everything. *He said that if all that was changed, then he'd be happy.*"

"Did you think he was right?"

"No. The reason was the same as all the others. Happiness doesn't depend on what is happening in the world; it depends on your perception of it. People can be happy if they desire it."

The Man smiled at David. "You have learned much, my young friend. You have done exactly what was required of you."

David frowned ever so slightly. "But I still don't understand what the picture means exactly. I think I know a little bit, but I don't know everything. That's what I was supposed to learn, wasn't it?"

"Yes, you were. And you have learned it. Take the scroll and spread it in front of you." David did.

The Man said, "Tell me, what do you see in the first picture?"

"I see *Iktumi* about to be eaten by an eagle."

"Do you know anything about *Iktumi* and the eagle?"

"Yes, but not too much. *Iktumi* is a trickster spider. He uses tricks to influence others. He's a liar. Our creator speaks to us and to all men through the eagle. The eagle is truth."

"Good. Now, what does your journey have in common with *Iktumi*?"

David looked at the picture for a moment. He knew he would never have been able to answer the question without his sister's help. When he closed his eyes to think about the question, he could hear her whisper the truth in his ears. To anyone else, it would have sounded like the wind. He answered, "*Iktumi* has eight legs, and I have eight different ways to be happy."

"Are they true ways to be happy?"

"They seem real enough to the people, but . . . "

David paused for a moment. He heard the word *no* whispered in his ear, and the reasons suddenly became clear. He spoke excitedly and quickly—the truth was beautiful to behold.

"But they aren't true! Each and every person seemed to need something different to be happy. Money, fame, relationships—they were all mentioned, but I could think of countless examples that showed them to be untrue. These are lies *Iktumi* uses to influence a person's mind! *Iktumi* doesn't want people

to be happy. He wants to teach them that happiness is always out of reach. *Iktumi* is very bad."

The Man nodded in agreement. "The tricks and lies of the spider have led many people away from the truth. I hope no one believes these lies because they can do nothing but keep you from being happy. Now, how are you represented in the picture?"

"By the eagle?"

"Exactly. Why?"

"Because I don't believe the lies of the spider! I have chosen to become the eagle, and I've decided to remove the lies from my life and replace them with truth."

The Man agreed. "The things *Iktumi* promises can't make a person happy. Instead, each and every person should replace the lies of *Iktumi* with the truth as you have done. The truth is beautiful and yet simple—*you alone are responsible for your happiness.* You alone control how you feel. You alone can make yourself happy. There's nothing else that can do it for you. You should also take the time to realize that you have many priceless treasures—things that you can completely call your own. Each and every one of us in this world has something to offer. Take the time to appreciate what you do have in your

life—don't focus on what you don't have. Realize that you, as well as all people, are the most special thing ever created. If you have nothing else, you have
life—a life you can choose to lead as you desire. A life where your dreams can
come true. *A life where you can be happy if you want to be, regardless of anything
that happens or doesn't happen to you.*"

The Man closed his eyes and began to think deeply for a moment. Then
slowly he began to recite a verse, one he had known since childhood. Even
though the Man spoke in Lakota, David was able to understand it.

> *In my youth I respected*
> *the world and life,*
> *I needed not anything but*
> *peace of heart,*
> *And yet I changed despite myself*
> *and believed in* Iktumi's *lies.*
> *He seemed to know all the truth,*
> *he promised to make me happy.*
> *He made me ask* Wakantanka *for wealth,*
> *that I might have power;*

I was given poverty, that I
    might find my inner strength.
I asked for fame,
    so others would know me;
I was given obscurity,
    that I might know myself.
I asked for a person to love that I
    might never be alone;
I was given the life of a hermit, that I
    might learn to accept myself.
I asked for power, that I
    might achieve;
I was given weakness, that I
    might learn to obey.
I asked for health, that I
    might lead a long life;
I was given infirmity, that I
    might appreciate each minute.

I asked Mother Earth for strength,
       that I might have my way;
I was given weakness, that I
       might feel the need for Her.
I asked to live happily, that I
       might enjoy life;
I was given life, that I might
       live happily.
I received nothing I asked for,
       yet all my wishes came true.
Despite myself and Iktumi,
       my dreams were fulfilled,
I am richly blessed
       more than I ever hoped.
I thank you, Wakantanka,
       for what you've given me.

David cried when the Man finished. They weren't tears of sadness, but tears of love and happiness. It affected him deeply—he knew he would remember it always.

The Man reached into his pocket and took out a new scroll. There was no writing on it. He began to list the eight lies of *Iktumi*.

THE EIGHT LIES OF *IKTUMI*

1. If only I were rich, then I'd be happy.

2. If only I were famous, then I'd be happy.

3. If only I could find the right person to marry, then I'd be happy.

4. If only I had more friends, then I'd be happy.

5. If only I were more attractive, then I'd be happy.

6. If only I weren't physically handicapped in any way, then I'd be happy.

7. If only someone close to me hadn't died, then I'd
    be happy.

8. If only the world were a better place, then I'd be
    happy.

NONE OF THESE THINGS ARE TRUE! WORK ON REMOVING THESE LIES
FROM YOUR LIFE AND YOU'LL FIND IT EASIER TO BE HAPPY. YOU CAN BE
HAPPY IF YOU WANT TO BE, AND THE FIRST STEP IS REMOVING THE LIES OF
IKTUMI FROM YOUR LIFE.

❧ The Lesson of the Drawing Man ❧
The Meaning of the Second Picture

YOU MUST UNDERSTAND THE MEANING OF HAPPINESS BEFORE YOU CAN BE HAPPY. AS WITH ANY JOURNEY, YOU CAN'T FIND THE END UNLESS YOU KNOW WHERE YOU'RE GOING. HAPPINESS, ALTHOUGH MISUNDERSTOOD BY MANY PEOPLE, IS NOT SOMETHING THAT IS DIFFICULT TO INCORPORATE INTO YOUR LIFE. ONCE YOU UNDERSTAND WHAT IT IS, YOU'LL BE ABLE TO IMPROVE EVERY ASPECT OF YOUR LIFE.

D avid watched the Man in wonder as he wrote the eight lies of *Iktumi*. He was very pleased that he had come to see him. He had learned so much in the past week—he had seen his sister in a vision, and he had felt the influx of knowledge into his heart. He was beginning to understand the meaning of life; he was beginning to understand himself.

He smiled as he looked at *Tunkasila*. As he did, he wondered about him. Where had he come from? And when? How old was he? There was so little he knew about him.

David assumed that these things were unimportant now. Instead, the Man *himself* was important. He was all David could ever hope to become; he was the person who could teach him to be happy. As he watched *Tunkasila*, he thought that he'd never seen a man so at peace with himself. *The way he looks and smiles, the way he sits and walks, brings an aura of strength to the words he speaks. I, too, wish to be like him,* David thought. *I wish to see the world with candid eyes that shield me from* Iktumi's *tricks. A man who sees the world in this way is a man who has conquered himself, made peace with his soul, and as a result is always happy. I too will conquer myself. I too will learn what it means to be happy so I will feel peace like he does.*

The Man lowered his eyes and sighed as he stopped writing. The candle flickered, and the Man began to sway back and forth slowly.

Minutes passed by, scores of minutes passed by, and still the Man swayed. The tea David drank was making him feel strange, almost light-headed.

He found himself mimicking *Tunkasila,* swaying in rhythm with him. He couldn't stop—it was as if strange forces were making him do it. The tea was taking effect—he began to lose the thoughts of himself, yet he was not afraid. He knew what it meant.

He was becoming the Man's shadow, a shadow of the Man's life and knowledge. It was the Indian way of achieving wisdom, and David knew enough not to stop the feelings and sensations that came with it.

The mimicking continued.

David closed his eyes at precisely the same moment that the Man closed his, and David listened to the quiet sounds of nature. A wolf howling in the distance, a leaf rustling in the wind, an eagle flapping its wings—these were the sounds that reached his ears. In his thoughts, David became the wolf, he became the leaf, and he became the eagle. He floated free from his body and became one with nature. He could feel the peace and tranquility of the circle of creation in which all is connected. David had never felt this way before— he had known about it but had never been part of it. For the first time, he was connected to all of nature's truth and beauty.

The Man began to chant softly. David couldn't understand the words— he was not man any longer. He was beyond the confines of human existence.

He was all things at once. As the chanting continued, David listened to it. It sounded strange—both melodic and peaceful at the same time. David found himself drawn into its hypnotic power.

Chanting.

Chanting.

And David was gone. He was no longer the wolf; he was no longer a leaf; he was no longer an eagle. He was something powerful and unknown. He was empty, yet he felt no fear. He was a deep void that needed to be filled.

Then there was light—a pinpoint of light far in the distance. A bright light. The light began to grow and move closer and closer. It brightened the darkness, and soon all was lit. The light enveloped him.

Chanting.

Chanting.

David allowed himself to become the light. It quenched a deep thirst he had never known he had. The light filled him with peace, tranquility, and knowledge. At first, the knowledge came in bits and pieces. David had trouble grasping the truth. After a few moments, the information began to take form. As it did, David began to grow brighter. The light was David, and David was the light. He knew he had learned the real meaning of happiness. Never before had it been so clear to him. He understood it from the depths of his heart and soul.

David opened his eyes and saw himself. David had become the Man; he had completed the circle. He was the teacher, he was *Tunkasila,* he lived in the heart of everything that is.

Chanting.

Chanting.

He closed his eyes, and David became himself again. But he retained a piece of the Man's knowledge. And a piece of the light. He knew the meaning of the second picture.

The chanting stopped.

David looked to the scroll. The second picture was that of a man looking toward the sun and drawing a picture of it in the sand. It signified understanding. *A man must understand what he is seeking before he can find it.* It must be very clear or the journey will have as its end the beginning. He would know no more than when he started.

David realized that happiness is a world of its own—a world that can be found in each and every one of us. It's an emotion that comes from the heart, one that can't be explained with mere words and phrases. And because this emotion is internal, there's nothing external that can make a person happy. External cures for happiness are one and the same as the tricks of *Iktumi*. That, of course, was the meaning of the light David had seen in his vision—when the light was external, he felt empty, and when the light came from inside him, he felt peace. Happiness, then, was simply a state of mind, a state that a person can control completely—whether things are going well or not. And contrary to what he had previously thought, the world of happiness is open to all those who desire it, and it can be a permanent part of one's life.

The truth was simple and beautiful. David thought for a long time about its meaning. The Man asked, "Have you found the meaning of the second picture?"

It took a moment for David to answer. "Yes, I think I have. It has many parts to it, but they're all connected. As I reflect on its meaning, I find that something has left me, like the old skin a snake sheds. Yet the new skin is much more beautiful and will allow me to grow in knowledge as well as stature."

David had trouble believing that it was he who was speaking. He had never spoken in such a way before. It was as if something—or someone—else was doing it for him. He was speaking as the Man would speak. He was speaking as his *ate* would speak. He was speaking as a teacher.

Or was the teacher speaking as a boy?

"Tell me," the Man asked, "what does *happiness* mean?"

"Happiness is an emotion that makes me feel good about myself. To be happy, I don't need one of *Iktumi's* tricks. I don't need light in the distance. I simply need desire and the knowledge of how to be happy. With desire and knowledge comes an internal light—a light of happiness—a light that leads me to strength, peace, and love. And if I believe and learn to be happy, I can be happy forever because I alone control it."

The Man nodded. "You've broken happiness down into distinct parts. Let's write each part so you'll never forget them."

The Man started to write on the new scroll again.

THE MEANING OF HAPPINESS

❀ *Happiness is an emotion that makes you feel a certain way.*

Happiness is an emotion just like the other emotions you have. Like all emotions, it's a very personal feeling—people can feel different when they're happy. It's important for you to recognize how you feel, and know when you're happy.

> ❀ *Happiness is a feeling that comes from within you,*
> *and is something only you can control.*

The feeling of happiness comes from within you. It doesn't come from somewhere else because it's an emotion—an internal feeling. In other words, each and every time you're happy, you alone are responsible. No one can take the credit for making you happy—the feeling is completely determined by you.

> ❀ *Happiness doesn't depend on external events.*

Happiness doesn't depend on what does happen or what doesn't happen to you. You learned that as soon as you rejected the eight lies of *Iktumi*. If you accept this statement and believe you can be happy no matter what, you'll find every aspect of your life improved.

❀ *You must learn to be happy.*

You must learn to be happy. You must take active steps to convince your mind that you are happy. Once you do, you can control this emotion to make your life better. If you learn how to be happy, you'll be able to be happy whenever you want to be.

❀ *You must desire happiness.*

You must have a desire for happiness in order to be happy. Without a desire for happiness, your mind will not allow you to be happy. But once the desire is there, nothing will keep it from taking root in your life.

❀ *Happiness can be a permanent feeling in your life.*

If you believe the other aspects of happiness, you'll realize you can be happy all the time! Not once in a while, not when things go right, but all the time. You'll feel happy the rest of your life.

✺ The Lesson of Fire ✺
The Meaning of the Third Picture

HAPPINESS SHOULD BE YOUR PERSONAL GOAL. IT SHOULD TRANSCEND ALL OTHER GOALS YOU HAVE IN YOUR LIFE. IF YOU ARE HAPPY, YOUR LIFE IS IMPROVED IN EVERY WAY. IT'S THE MOST POWERFUL FORM OF POSITIVE THINKING. WITH IT, ALL YOUR GOALS CAN BE REALIZED.

It took a long time for the Man to write the meaning of happiness. As David reflected on what was written, he knew it was true. It made him feel good that feeling happy was completely up to him. What, then, was the meaning of the third picture?

David looked to the scroll again. It was a picture of a man using a fire to warm his hands and cook his food.

The Man said, "Tell me what you see in the third picture."

"I see a man using fire."

"Tell me, how does that relate to your desire to learn how to be happy?"

David closed his eyes, and the answer came to him. It did not come right away—in fact, it took David a long time to understand. The answers came in the form of whispering winds, short bursts of natural energy that flowed into him, controlled him, and led him to the truth. He knew it was his sister again. Even in death, she would not leave him. She was part of nature and was using nature to communicate with him. David opened his eyes after she had left him; he had no idea he had been quiet for over an hour.

"I suppose that this picture provides the meaning of happiness in my life. Put simply, it tells me why I should be happy."

The Man nodded. He was impressed that the young Indian was learning so quickly. Then: "How is happiness represented in the picture?"

"By the fire. The man is using it for a number of things."

"Good things, or bad things?"

"Good things. He is using it to cook and to stay warm."

"Are these things necessary to live?"

"Well, a person can't live without eating, or if it is too cold. He can live, however, without fire. His meat would be raw, and he would have to wear heavy skins to keep warm."

"Is this a good thing, or is this a bad thing?"

"His life is much worse when he doesn't have fire, so I suppose it is a bad thing."

"Relate it to happiness for me."

"Well, you don't need to be happy to live, but it improves every aspect of your life. With happiness, you can do many things—just as you can use fire to do many things. *Happiness is the best way to lead the kind of life you desire."*

"Good. Now how else can fire be related to happiness?"

"Well, you have to feed the fire to keep it burning. Otherwise it will go out. *In the same way, you can't be happy all the time unless you have learned to be happy, and work on it."*

"Do you have to work every minute of your life to be happy all the time?"

"No. *Just as you don't have to feed the fire continually, you don't have to work all the time to be happy.* Only when the fire is getting low do you need to feed it again. The same thing can be said of happiness."

"Good. Answer me this, then—does a fire burn better when you only feed it when it is low, or when you add fuel even when it is burning well?"

"It would burn better if you add fuel even while it is burning well."

"Can anything external put the fire out?"

"Not if the person who has the fire tries hard enough to keep it lit. He can cover the flames if it rains; he can shelter the flames if it's windy. In fact, fire was coveted by our ancestors. They kept it burning for years at a time. Nothing would extinguish the flames. It was the responsibility of the tribe to keep it burning at all times, through winter and summer."

"You are getting very close. There's only one more thing you need to understand. Tell me, how else can you relate fire and happiness?"

It took a long time before David answered. He said, *"Fire is either there or it isn't.* You can't *almost* have a fire—you either have a flame or you don't. The same thing can be said of happiness. *You're either happy or you're not happy.* You can't be partially happy—it's impossible."

The Man looked up for a moment and smiled. "I am pleased with what you have learned so far. You are becoming very wise."

David had never been called that before. He was becoming like his *ate*— a man he greatly admired. He said humbly, "I feel I still have a long way to go."

"The path is actually very short. Now that you understand what the picture signifies, our next step is to understand the purpose of the fire and why it is important in your life."

"Or why happiness is important in a person's life?"

The Man nodded, then closed his eyes before he began. "Happiness is a wonderful feeling. There's nothing in this world that can make you feel so good about your life. *Like light and dark, however, happiness has an opposite.* It goes by many names in many languages. I'm sure you've heard of it before. In our language it's called *cantesica*. The *Wasicu* may call it despair. It's a feeling of sorrow about who you are and what you do. It will ruin your life. It's one of the most destructive forces in nature, a force so powerful that thousands of people have been killed by it. *Cantesica* leads you to death."

David shivered. He suddenly felt cold. He had never seen a person so frightened of an emotion. He leaned forward and listened to the Man carefully.

"*Cantesica* will destroy you because it tricks you like *Iktumi*. It's the mirrored image of happiness, an exact opposite that leads to destruction. Like happiness, it too is learned, it comes from within you, and it's something only you control. It can become a permanent way of life if you desire it. And because of this, it's very dangerous. It leads you to believe you have nothing to live for. It brings about feelings of loneliness, anger, hatred, and resentment. It's also very dangerous because it shifts the blame for your problems to someone else and prevents you from being happy again because the truth is hidden from you. Despair is like a harmful, addictive drug: it takes over your life, controls what you do, and eventually ruins you."

David had never thought of it in those terms. *Cantesica* can enter a man's life in many ways. He would never allow it to happen to him again. As the Man finished, David thought of his sister. Suddenly, he knew why she had been visiting him! This was the truth she had wanted him to find. He had been feeling despair—and she who was beyond this world knew that despair would destroy him in time. That's why she was leading him to find the answers. David smiled to himself. "My sister wants me to be happy."

The Man nodded. "She is your protector. She desires happiness for you because it alone will save your life in times of trouble. Happiness will make you feel good about yourself and other people. You'll find that your feelings of happiness transcend your life and everything you do."

David listened as the Man described why happiness is important.

"Happiness will reduce stress in your life because you can adjust to any problems in a positive way. This in turn makes you physically healthier."

The Man paused for a moment, a smile on his face as he looked upward. It was clear to David that he was seeing the face of a Man who has honored *Wakantanka* with happiness and love of life.

The Man went on. "You see, happiness enables you to change your life for the better. If you're happy, you react to the bad things in your life in a different way. Happiness makes you work positively to improve your situation. Happiness also creates enthusiasm, which provides additional energy in everything you do. If you combine this enthusiasm with desire, faith, and persistence, you'll have a way to reach your personal goals no matter what they are. In total, if you're happy, *everything in your life is improved.* Happiness is both the beginning and end of all the goals you have in your life. And most important, *it's the most wonderful feeling in the world.*"

He paused for a moment. "Let me tell you something I once read that tells the importance of happiness in your life:

"Every morning you are handed twenty-four golden hours. They are one of the few things in this world that you get free of charge. If you had all the money in the world, you couldn't buy an extra hour. What will you do with your priceless treasure? Remember, you must use it, as it is given only once. Once wasted, you cannot get it back."

The Man continued. "The importance of a happy life can't be exaggerated. Think of each and every day as priceless. If you take a series of those days and combine them, it becomes a year. Add the years together, and it becomes a lifetime—a lifetime of love, happiness, honor, hopes, and dreams. If you're happy every day, when it's time to leave this earth, you'll have led a happy life. That's all anyone could hope for."

The Man took the new scroll and began to list the reasons why feeling sorry for yourself is bad and feeling happy is good. He wrote them in the spot where the third picture was on David's scroll.

WHY YOU SHOULD NEVER FEEL DESPAIR

Feeling despair or unhappiness:

* ❈ *makes you feel anger, loneliness, and resentment.*

* ❈ *can't solve your problems, and in fact stops you from solving them.*

* ❈ *often creates new problems.*

🌸 *limits friendships with other people.*

🌸 *has no positive benefits.*

🌸 *will eventually destroy your life.*

**AND, MOST OF ALL, YOU DON'T HAVE TO FEEL DESPAIR!
AS WITH HAPPINESS, IT'S ALL UP TO YOU!**

WHY IT'S IMPORTANT TO BE HAPPY

When you are happy:

🌸 *you feel good. You feel joy, peace, cheer, and contentment.*

🌸 *you are pleased with who you are and what you do.*

🌸 *people enjoy being around you.*

🌸 *you have higher self-esteem.*

🌸 *your life is improved physically.*

🌸 *you can more easily solve any problems that may arise.*

🌸 *you have additional energy.*

🌸 *your life is improved in every way.*

🌸 *you will be honoring* Wakantanka *with His most precious gift to you.*

YOU HAVE THE BEST POSSIBLE LIFE IMAGINABLE—A HAPPY ONE!

❦ The Lesson of a Man ❦
Sitting Beneath a Tree

The Meaning of the Fourth Picture

HAPPINESS IS SOMETHING EACH OF US CAN LEARN TO CONTROL. THE SECRET
IS KNOWING HOW. AFTER LEARNING THE MEANING OF THE FOURTH PICTURE,
YOU WILL KNOW THE GREATEST SECRET IN THE WORLD—HOW TO BE HAPPY
EACH AND EVERY DAY OF YOUR LIFE.

Because it was late, the two decided to rest. David had learned more than he ever thought he would, and he was exhausted. The Man showed him to his room, and David went to sleep almost immediately. That night, David had a dream:

He found himself in a great desert. White sand, long bleached by the burning rays of the sun, stretched as far as the eye could see. It was to the horizon that David needed to go, but he knew he wouldn't make it. His tongue was swollen and dry, coated in dust, cracked and bleeding. His arms were swollen from the burns the sun caused, his eyes ached from the brightness of the desert, and his legs wobbled beneath him. He felt dry inside and out. His body told him to stop, to rest, to wait until nightfall to continue his journey. But consciously he knew there would be no nightfall.

He was in the Desert of Loneliness, a place where nightfall never came.

It was a place of despair, of sadness. The sun never stopped shining, the winds were never at your back, the sand never hardened, and the horizon was never reached. It was a life of living hell, a life where pain became common, and hope for the future was nonexistent. David knew he couldn't fight the desert any more than he could fight with any other aspect of Mother Earth. In the end, it would take him as it had taken all others before him. He would die soon, he knew that, and he was afraid, although it was not due to his approaching death.

David was frightened by the fact that he didn't care one way or the other whether he died. Life had as much meaning as death; he had no feelings of hope for the future. Why did he not care if he died? Why didn't he long for life anymore? David knew these thoughts were the things that were destroying him, but he couldn't stop them. That's why he was frightened. He was out of control; he had given up his life to the feelings of sorrow.

David's knees buckled, and he fell to the sand. He knew he would not get up. There was nothing left to keep him going. He had used all his strength and was ready to die here.

As the sun beat down, the Man in the Hills appeared. He stood over David, his white hair blowing in the wind, and David felt immediately that the Man had come to help him. But as David looked to him, his feelings began to change. The Man's arms hung loosely at his sides as if he were very tired, his shoulders no longer seemed as broad as they had been in the past, and his face looked weather-beaten and aged. There was nothing extraordinary about the Man anymore—he was simply an old Indian standing in the desert. But why? What had happened to him?

The answer came a few moments later. David came to the realization that he saw sadness in the Man's eyes—sadness was killing the Man. It was tiring him, making him age with weakness, and would surely kill him within hours. The thought of that made David feel worse. Even the Man could not be happy in this desert. *David coughed up some sand that had trickled down his throat. Then he spoke in a raspy tone. "Why have you come?"*

"I've come because I was needed," the Man answered.

"You're here to help me?"

The Man nodded. He did not offer his hand. David coughed again. This time the cough cut the back of his parched throat. "Do you have water? I need water. That's the only thing that can help me now."

The Man looked around in confusion. He sighed, then answered after a few moments, "There's water all around you. Can you not see it?"

"There's no water," David wheezed.

"If you can't see it, you'll never find it," the Man answered as he shook his head. He stood over David for a few more seconds, then turned and started to walk away. Because his throat was so dry, David couldn't say anything. All he could do was raise his head and watch

the Man vanish into the hot air of the desert.

David closed his eyes. He had felt the Man's presence beside him and had been left alone. He had not been helped. Yet, the Man's appearance had brought him to think of his life and its meaning. Did anything have meaning in his life?

Yes, he knew of one thing.

His thoughts turned to his dog. David was only three when Korak was brought home. They grew up together. For years, Korak had watched over him. He led David to safety in times of danger, he helped David find his way when he was lost. Now, Korak was getting older. His back legs were arthritic, and sometimes David needed to help him get up the stairs. His dog needed him now—David had to keep him safe. It was something only David could do because the dog was his and his alone. For just a moment, David smiled. He would give anything just to see his dog one more time.

Suddenly and without warning, the rains came.

David woke up just as the sun was rising. He didn't immediately realize where he was and felt disoriented as he rolled over. When he sat up and looked outside, he saw the Man working in the garden. David smiled. There was something about the Man that made him very special. He wondered what he would learn today.

The Man stood and stretched his hands to the sun. He knew David was awake and began walking toward the house. David emerged just as the Man approached the door.

"Come," the Man said with a smile, "we must learn from Mother Earth today."

The two walked in silence for a long while. From time to time, David's thoughts turned to his sister, but he no longer felt despair. He missed her greatly and loved her with all his heart, but he knew she was with him, teaching him and leading him to happiness.

And most of all, she *was* helping him feel better! For the first time in a long while, he felt himself regaining control of his life. She had helped him learn the lessons of the first three pictures on the scroll, and he had no doubt he would learn the lessons of the rest of them. His father had been right— the scroll could indeed teach him everything he needed to know about being happy. He was thankful she was there to guide him to the truth.

More than that, however, David felt better for another reason. He knew he had been in the company of a person who would change his life forever—although he wasn't sure how. Last night was just an example—the first of many, David knew. The Man had entered his dream and saved him. But why? Could it be that David only felt better now, but the feeling wouldn't last after he left here? Or was the Man David's new Guardian Angel? Or worse, did *Wakantanka* believe David wouldn't be able to overcome his despair? David wasn't sure, but he came to a decision about how he would deal with these thoughts. He would stay here and learn from the Man until he could learn no more. He would learn how to lead his life, how to think, how to act, how to help—how to do anything that made him more like the Man. He would learn from nature, and he would learn from watching the Man walk and listening to him talk. He would learn in the same way his father had been taught. He would hear his forefathers' souls in the winds; he would learn from the sun, the rivers, the seasons, and from all of nature's creatures. And somewhere along the way, David knew he would learn to be happy.

The Man slowed his gait and stopped after a few steps. He bent toward the ground and picked up an acorn. David watched him as the Man turned it in his hand. His expression was clearly that of awe. But why? There were thousands of acorns on the ground. Why had he singled out this one?

The Man handed the acorn to David.

"What is it?" he asked David.

David looked at it as it sat in his hand. He realized that the Man knew it was an acorn. Still, David also knew that calling it an acorn wasn't the real answer the Man wanted. He wanted more.

"I don't know."

The Man smiled. "It's an acorn. It is the fruit of the oak tree, the fruit from which the mighty oak grows."

David looked at his hand. "I know what it is, but I don't know what it means or why you asked. I've come to know you, and I know you often want an answer that I'm unable to give. I know I've come to learn *from* Mother Earth today; I've not come to learn *about* Mother Earth."

David felt dizzy for a second. The words that came from him moments before were not his own—his sister must have put those thoughts in his mind.

The Man smiled. "You're right. You'll learn *from* Her, not *about* Her. Today, you'll learn the secret of happiness. Mother Earth has told you the secret a thousand times, but today you'll listen to her. She will show you how to wake up every day with a smile and laugh at the problems that confront you. You'll become like your father, and in time, you'll teach your son the things you have learned."

David looked back at the acorn. He never knew he could learn these things from it, but then again, he had doubted that his father had learned the things he knew from nature.

The Man reached over and took it from him. "Now," he said again, "what can you learn from the acorn?"

"The greatest secret in the world?" David asked.

"Yes," the Man said as he smiled and held it for David to see. "This acorn is the seed of the oak tree. It is small and fragile now—even the squirrels can destroy it. Yet if the acorn is left unharmed, in time it will grow to be something very strong and powerful. The acorn is the oak tree of the future—it is the first step in the long process of the tree's growth."

"How does it relate to my life and happiness?"

"Take the scroll from your pocket and look at the fourth picture."

David did. He saw a man sitting under an oak tree. There was a pile of acorns beside him, and the man in the picture appeared to be meditating.

"The tree in the picture you see shows you the secret of happiness, and the man in the picture shows you how to use this secret to be happy."

David studied the picture. He did not see how he could learn these things just from looking at it. The Man went on.

"To understand the importance of the picture, you must learn from nature. Look around you. Look at the sky, the wildlife, and the creatures of Mother Earth. Think about what you see, and answer these questions for yourself. Do you see mystery all around you? Do you wonder about the world and what *Wakantanka* has created? And most important, do you think *Wakantanka* created the world without order?"

David looked around. What he saw was a mysterious, well-planned world. The sky fed the earth with rain, the winds fed the earth by moving seeds. The creatures used the earth to eat and find shelter. There was no randomness here. The world was indeed created with order. He could think of nothing that could be taken away from the earth and not have an effect.

"Now think of the seasons," the Man went on. "Can you change the order of the seasons, or does spring always follow winter? Does autumn always follow summer, or can you change the sequence of Mother Earth?"

"No," David said as he shook his head. He still didn't know what the Man was leading up to.

"Now answer me this—do animals age backwards? Does the oak tree grow smaller with the passage of time? Does the rain fall before the clouds appear?"

"No, of course not," David answered as he wondered what it meant.

"Now, think of the acorn with these questions and answers in mind. How does the acorn grow into a tree? The acorn must fall from the tree, then it finds its way into the ground. It must be watered and left unharmed while it sprouts. If these things are done, the tree will grow. Acorns will fall from it over the years, and more trees will grow. After a hundred years, the tree will grow old and die. Just as there are sequences in nature—the seasons, for example—a tree has a sequence, too, and it can't be changed. There is no way that the tree can grow smaller with age because it is not the tree's sequence. There is no way that this acorn can produce acorns now because it is not the tree's sequence. There is no way that the tree can die first and then grow because it is not the tree's sequence."

"What does that mean to me?"

"The tree in the picture represents the sequence in your life. Like the tree, you are born. You are small at first, but if cared for properly, you will grow to be a man. Once a man, you can produce offspring. After a hundred years, you will die. That is your life sequence. You can't change the sequence, because it is part of the order of Mother Earth. Do you understand what I've told you?"

"Yes, I think so, but I still don't see how it can make me happy."

The Man smiled. "Like the acorn and yourself, *happiness has sequences, too.* As you've learned, happiness comes from within you, not from something that happens. This means that whenever you're happy, it is because you have completed a sequence of things that made you happy. The sequence cannot be broken or changed, because it is the way of Mother Earth."

The Man paused and placed his hand on David's shoulder.

"You'll be happy when you use the sequence of happiness. Once you learn the sequence, you can use it whenever you want to be happy. If your desire is to be happy all the time, then you'll use the sequence every day. That is why your father is always happy—he uses a sequence of happiness."

"Why does it work?"

The Man shrugged his shoulders as he answered. "Why do trees grow in sequence? Why do *you* grow in sequence? *It is the order of Mother Earth.* She has designed the world with order, and you are part of Her design. There is order in your life—there are sequences in everything you do. You know that if you're hungry, you must eat. You don't eat then become hungry. That would be out of sequence."

David looked at the scroll again. He thought about sequences in his life. He thought of growing tired and going to bed. Could he change that sequence? No, he knew he couldn't. He then thought of exercising. Could he grow tired before exercising? Again, the answer was no. David thought deeply for a long while about everything he did during the course of the day. Each and every thing had its own sequence. It was like what the Man had said about the order of the world—just as spring always follows winter and autumn always follows summer—there is always a certain sequence of events that never changes.

But did happiness really have a sequence, too? Yes, deep down, he knew it did. He knew the Man would tell him about the sequence, and he was pleased that he had learned his father's secret. He was anxious to use it in his own life.

David looked at the scroll again and stared at the man sitting under the tree. Learning the secret of how to be happy was David's reason for coming to see the Man. No doubt this would be the most important lesson of all.

The Man walked to a nearby tree and sat under it. David followed and sat across from the Man.

"Can you tell me the secret of the man in the picture?" David asked.

The Man nodded. "Of course. That's why you've come to me."

The Man smiled and closed his eyes for a moment. Then he began: "Happiness comes from inside you, David. Your mind—not anything else—is the only thing that will make you happy. This means that you can learn to use your mind to make you happy even when things are going wrong. To do this, you'll simply use a sequence of thoughts and actions. It's very simple to do, and I promise that it works. *Believe in this picture, and you will know how to be happy.*"

"I will, I promise. I've seen how it helps my father and I've seen how it helps you."

"Good. You're ready to learn the greatest secret in the world."

He paused for a moment.

"David, the man in the picture is meditating. He is sitting in the womb of Mother Earth because he feels most comfortable there. He is touching the soil, drawing strength from Mother Earth. You, however, can do this meditation wherever you're comfortable. You must do it three times a day—each and every day of your life. Are you willing to do this?"

"Yes," David said as he nodded, "I'd do anything to be happy all the time."

"Then let's discuss what the man in the picture is doing. First, he is thinking about something that makes him happy. Second, he is telling himself that he is happy."

He paused for a moment. *"That, my young friend, is the secret of happiness."*

It took a few moments for David to respond.

"That's all?" David finally asked. For some reason, he had expected the secret to be more difficult.

"Yes, that's all there is to it. You're wondering why it works, aren't you?"

"Yes," David said after a moment.

"It's very simple. First, remember the sequences. Just as summer follows spring, you will be happy if you do these two things while you meditate. You can no more change the order of the seasons than you can stop this meditation from working. Why does it work? It works because you're convincing yourself that you're happy."

He stopped again and picked up a stick that was sitting on the ground. He began to sketch the fourth picture in the dirt while he spoke.

"You see, whenever you feel happy, it's because you've convinced yourself that you should feel that way. Remember, the feeling comes from within you. By thinking happy thoughts, you're making your mind focus on things that make you feel good. By telling yourself that you're happy, the words become truth in your life. The words and thoughts enter your subconscious mind—the mind that often causes you to act in ways that you don't understand. Even if you don't believe the meditation works, it will still make you happy. You're using a sequence of happiness, a sequence that cannot be changed. The end result will be achieved. The sequence always works, and you'll be happy."

"What should I think of during the meditation?"

"Anything that makes you happy. Think of playing with your friends, think of a recent trip, think of a person you love. Think back to an experience that made you feel good, and think of it in detail. Use all the senses possible when you think of it. See the event, hear the event, smell the event, and feel it in your thoughts. Your mind will think it is real. Then, tell yourself that you're happy. Say out loud, 'I am happy.' When you've done this, the sequence will be completed, and you will be happy."

The Man went on. "I meditate three times a day, each and every day of my life. I think happy thoughts and tell myself I am happy. It has become habit in my life, and as a result, I am habitually happy. I've replaced bad habits with good habits, and I've led a wonderful life as a result."

David thought for a moment. Could it be true? Yes, it must be true. It is the way of Mother Earth and *Wakantanka*.

The Man went on. "To meditate, find a comfortable place where you won't be disturbed. Then close your eyes and relax. Count to ten, exhaling as you do so. Relax further with each breath. Once you reach ten, take a moment to feel what you are experiencing. Then begin to think of something that makes you happy. Use all your senses to make it real in your mind. Tell yourself you're happy. Say it aloud ten times. Once you've done this, count from ten back to one, open your eyes, and smile. You will be happy—you will feel very good. The feeling may only last for a moment, but don't worry. That's typical in the beginning. The more you do the exercise, the easier it will be to be happy all the time."

The Man took out the new scroll and began to write the meaning of the fourth picture.

THE SECRET OF HAPPINESS

❀ *There are sequences in everything you do.*

❀ *You will use a sequence to make yourself happy.*

❀ *The sequence always works. You will be happy when you are finished.*

❀ *If you think happy thoughts, you will be happy because you convince your mind that you feel good.*

❀ *To be happy, meditate quietly three times a day. Relax so you can communicate with your subconscious mind.*

❀ *When you meditate, think happy thoughts and tell yourself that you're happy.*

THE MEDITATION EXERCISE
(Do this three times a day)

1. Find a comfortable place to relax.

2. Close your eyes and count from one to ten, exhaling with each number.

3. Relax further as the count progresses.

4. Once you reach ten, feel the relaxation spread through your body.

5. Think of anything that makes you happy. Make it as real as possible.

6. Say aloud ten times, "I am happy."

7. Count from ten back to one and open your eyes.

8. Smile.

IF YOU DO THIS, YOU'LL BE HAPPY. IF YOU DO IT EVERY DAY, YOU'LL FIND THAT YOU'RE HAPPY ALL THE TIME. HAPPINESS WILL BE A HABITUAL FEELING FOR YOU.

∞ The Lesson of Sticks ∞
The Meaning of the Fifth Picture

YOUR HAPPINESS IS LARGELY DEPENDENT ON THE WAY YOU VIEW YOURSELF AND THE WORLD AROUND YOU. TO BE HAPPY, YOU MUST VIEW YOURSELF AND THE WORLD AROUND YOU AS SOMETHING VERY SPECIAL. THIS PICTURE DISCUSSES THE TEN TRUTHS OF HAPPINESS. IF YOU WANT TO HAVE A BETTER LIFE AND IMPROVE EVERYTHING YOU DO, MASTER THE TEN OUTLOOKS. YOU'LL FIND YOU'VE BECOME A BETTER, HAPPIER PERSON.

The First Cycle of the Moon

After the Man had finished writing the meaning of the fourth picture, the two rose from the shade of the tree and took a walk. David thought about it for a long while. While he walked, he thought about his sister and the fun they used to have together. Although he didn't tell himself that he was happy, the pleasant thoughts of them playing together made him feel better. He couldn't help but smile. More important, David also knew why he had been feeling so depressed over his sister's death. In the same way that sequences can be used to make him happy, they had been used to make him feel sad. David had been thinking of the funeral, or the moment when he first knew she had died, or how much he would miss her in the future. He had been thinking of things that hurt him greatly. He couldn't help but feel horrible. From that point on, he wouldn't think of those things. When he thought of his sister, he would think only of their fun times together or her spirit flying free. These thoughts would help him feel good.

As the two walked, David also looked at the wonder of Mother Earth. She was beautiful and peaceful—and a great teacher. Perhaps she could help him with the question he was thinking about now, a question that bothered him greatly.

The Man had told him that he could be happy if he meditated. He knew it was true . . . but isn't there something else to the feeling of happiness? Yes, David thought so. To him, happiness isn't just a feeling, it's a way of looking at the world. When David looked at the Man, he saw peace and contentment on his face. There was strength, beauty, and softness in the Man's movements. David believed that while meditation helped, the Man's happiness was fueled by the way he looked at the world and the way he lived his life. He took pleasure in everything he did and saw.

But how?

This was the question David needed Mother Earth to answer. He wanted the answer very badly because he wished to be more like the Man. He wanted to see the world in the same way the Man did. That, too, David believed, is a secret of happiness.

The Man did not speak while David thought of these things.

After they had walked in silence for a long while, the Man spoke. "David, you look confused. Is there something I can do to help you?"

"I'm not sure. I've learned so much from you, but I feel that something is still missing from my life."

"What's that?"

"Well, I know I can be happy when I want to be, but I need something else in my life."

"Do you want to see the world with new eyes?"

David nodded.

"That, my friend, is the meaning of the next picture."

David turned to the Man.

"It is?"

The Man nodded.

"Yes. Happiness is a fire that needs to be fueled. You can meditate and feel good, but to have happiness transcend your life and everything you do, you must lead your life with certain beliefs. Just as you have rid your life of the eight lies of *Iktumi*, you must fill your life with ten absolute truths. These truths are the secret of a better life. If you lead your life with the ten truths and meditate daily, you will be happy. You'll see the world in a way you've never seen it before. You will appreciate all life, love all things, and have an unseen strength that will help you through any problems."

"What are the ten truths, and how will I learn them?"

"The ten truths are outlooks on life. They are quite simple to explain, but you must take the time to learn them. You must make them part of your life. *To learn them, you must master each of them one at a time. You must not proceed to the next outlook until you have mastered the one before it.* By doing this, they will not be forgotten."

"How long will this take?"

"It will take ten cycles of the moon—a little less than one year. You'll begin to learn an outlook with each new moon. You'll read the outlook on your new scroll three times each day during the cycle—read it immediately following your meditation. When the next new moon arrives, begin to master the following outlook. In less than a year, you'll have changed your life completely. *You'll have learned the secret of the ages; you'll have mastered yourself.* You'll become a teacher and will be sought by others who wish to learn from you."

David thought about the commitment. *Ten cycles of the moon?* That was a long time. Could he do it? He sat silently for quite a long time before he came to his answer. Yes, he knew, he would do it. He would master the outlooks because he could expect no less of himself. He has been given the key to a better life; he has been given the key to happiness. This is why he had come to *Paha Sapa.*

The Man spoke. "The outlooks will do much for you. Not only will they make you happy, they will improve everything you do. *Everything!* There is nothing as important in life as to do what I have asked."

"When do we begin?"

The Man smiled. "Look at the fifth picture on the scroll."

David saw a picture of a man using sticks to fuel a fire. There were ten of them. "What is the first outlook?"

"It is the most basic truth of all. It teaches you how wonderful you are. It helps you lead your life with love and hope. During the first cycle of the moon, I want you to lead your life—each and every day—with the belief that you are the most special thing ever created."

The Man cleared his throat. "Listen, learn, and say the following things to yourself three times a day. By the end of the cycle, you will believe them."

David began to write the first outlook on the new scroll.

REALIZE I AM THE MOST SPECIAL THING EVER CREATED
The First Stick Needed to Fuel the Fire of Happiness

Since long before the sun rose in the sky and even before Wakantanka *created the womb of Mother Earth in which we live, there has never been anyone exactly like me. No person in the past has had exactly my characteristics, my personality, or my abilities. No one has ever grown at the same rate, learned the same things, or wondered about life in the same way I have. Nor is there any worry that anyone ever will, because I can't be duplicated in the future. My place in history is secure because no one will ever be the same as me.*

I am the most special thing ever created.

Why am I so special? Because I have things that no one else can ever have. I am unique in this world, and no warrior or chief or common man can ever lay claim to the things I have. I alone have my thoughts and hopes. I alone have my beating heart, my stamina, and my love of life. Can anyone else lay claim to my dreams? Can anyone else love like me? Is there anyone who sees exactly the same color I do when I look at a budding flower? Has anyone before me ever heard the howl of a coyote with exactly the same pitch? Will anyone ever be able to duplicate my deeds and actions? No, I know these things are mine and mine alone. How can I not be happy with these thoughts in my heart and in my soul?

I am the most special thing ever created.

Because I am the most special thing ever created, I am valuable. Like a diamond, I am rare and beautiful. I am worth more than anything in the world. What good is money when compared to me? No money could ever buy my thoughts. What good is fame when compared to me? No amount of fame can make me more special. What good is any earthly item? None can be traded for me. My happiness is secured by this knowledge.

I am the most special thing ever created.

I know I shouldn't waste my life. I am here for a purpose. I am here to grow in wisdom. I am here to love all things. I am here to honor Wakantanka. How can I do these things? I can begin by being happy. I can be happy if I realize I am the most special thing ever created. If I am so special, I can surely smile with pride at who I am. I can be happy, I will be happy—I am happy.

I am happy because I am the most special thing ever created.

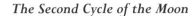
The Second Cycle of the Moon

It took a long time for David to write the outlook on his new scroll. He thought about its meaning in his life and came to the belief that this outlook was very important. He knew that his father lived his life with this attitude, and he would begin to use it in his own life. Each day after meditating, he would read the scroll. He would read it over and over until it became part of his soul.

When he finished, the Man began speaking about the second outlook. "There are many reasons why some people are happy and others are unhappy. One of the most obvious is that people who are unhappy feel that life has been unfair to them. They feel jealousy or anger when they compare their lives to those they admire. Instead, they should take the time to appreciate what life *has* given them."

He paused for a moment. "During the second cycle, I want you to take the time each day to appreciate what life has given you. Think of all the good things in your life and write them down. You'll find that you have many wonderful things. Think of those things each day, and you'll view the world in a better way. And most important, read the outlook on your new scroll after you meditate. Do it three times a day during the second cycle of the moon."

David wrote the new outlook as the Man spoke.

APPRECIATE WHAT LIFE HAS GIVEN ME
The Second Stick Needed to Fuel the Fire of Happiness

I will be happy because I appreciate what life has given me.
As I sit and wonder about the beauty of life, I come to believe that I am pleased with all that life has given me. Although I have not received everything I have wanted, I do not feel sadness, because it makes me love the things I have much more. If I had perfect health, would I appreciate a challenging walk? If I was incredibly beautiful, would I appreciate someone who thought I was attractive? If I had immense wealth, would I appreciate a gift given to me by a friend? No, I know it would be impossible. Because I know and accept this truth, I am able to understand why I have not been given everything I want. I am Wakantanka's *special child.* Wakantanka *knows I am strong*

enough not to think of what I don't have, but to appreciate what I do have. Thank you, Wakantanka, for having such faith in me.

I will appreciate what life has given me.

Instead of dwelling on what I do not have, today I will think of my mind and all it offers. It is the power of my mind that separates me from the animals and all others in the world. With it I can think of beauty and love. I can think of peace and fulfillment. What else can I do with my mind? Anything! I can fly like an eagle or run like a wolf. In my dreams, I never go hungry or grow tired. There are no bounds to my world, no limits to what I can accomplish. How I love this aspect of my life!

I will appreciate what life has given me.

I know it is my nature to want more than I will ever receive. It is part of my soul and separates me from other creatures. It is a strength I can use to better my life. I know there is nothing wrong with desires, dreams, ambitions, or wants because they fuel a fire that burns in me. Yet, deep down, I realize that none of the things I want in life can make me happy. Instead, to be happy, I must think of how many wonderful things I have now, at the present time. I must think that life itself is so incredibly special that I must not waste a minute dwelling on negative things. I must know that I am special, that all life is special, and that I am able to enjoy it now. I must know that I can be happy if none of my dreams come true, because all happiness takes is an appreciation of life.

I will appreciate what life has given me.

I know that happiness is both the beginning and end of my journey in life. I know that I must be happy in order to reach my goals, because negative thoughts would stop me long before I reached them. Yet, why do I have goals that I try to reach? So I can be happy! Happiness is a circular journey, one in which my end is my beginning. What does this mean? It means that I can feel good about myself whether or not I reach my goal. It means I don't need a reason to be happy. It means I can be happy all the time. These simple thoughts are enough to make me appreciate my life now.

I will appreciate what life has given me.

I have so many wonderful things. What do I have? I have life. I have an ability to love. I can think. I can dream. I can hope. I can pray. I can feel. I can breathe. I can smell. I can see. I can walk. I can talk. I can help. I can be happy. Only I can do these things for me. And if there are some things I cannot do or do not have, it doesn't matter, because I have the most precious gift of all. I have myself, and no one can ever take it from me.

I will appreciate what life has given me.

I will adjust to life accordingly. Life has given me so much that I don't need anything else. I know I can be happy because of this fact. I will adjust positively to the bad things that happen to me and be happy because of it. I will not expect all my goals or dreams to come true, but I will be happy! *Others may have more things than I,* but I will be happy! *Others may be more attractive,* but I will be happy! *And why will I be happy? Because I know and appreciate what life has given me. I am happy because I want to be happy. Life has given me the abili-*

ty to be happy, and to honor myself I will be happy. Like a circle. The end and the beginning. Happiness.

Thank you, life, for all you have given me.

The Third Cycle of the Moon

David enjoyed writing the second outlook. He knew this particular way of looking at the world was something his father did. If he did it, too, then he would be more like his father.

The Man waited until David had finished before he began with the third outlook.

"A happy person views his life with hope for the future. You should, too. If you view your life with optimism, you'll find it easy to be happy. You'll view your life as something exciting, challenging, and full of promise at the same time. After you've mastered the first two pictures, you'll begin to learn this outlook. This will take place during the third cycle of the moon. Read this outlook three times a day after you meditate."

David nodded and the Man began.

View Your Life with Optimism and Hope for the Future
The Third Stick Needed to Fuel the Fire of Happiness

I am happy because I view my life with optimism and hope for the future.

Little by little, everything adds up. A single drop of rain seems to make little difference in the world. Yet, as it flows downhill, it gathers with other drops, and soon a trickle develops. This trickle becomes a stream, a stream becomes a river, and soon the drop is part of something so powerful it cannot be stopped. I will lead my life in the same way. Optimism is a drop of rain, a belief that something good will happen to me today. At first the optimism may not seem important. I may forget about it, yet I know it stays with me. Then I will be optimistic about a second thing, and then a third. Like the drops that turned to a trickle, my optimism will grow stronger. Soon it will flow in my life and will not be stopped. Why will I do this? Why do I want to be optimistic? Because optimism is something that makes me happy. And I want to be happy.

I will view my life with optimism and hope for the future.

I have hope about my life because I know the future is unlimited for me. While the past is gone, only I can decide what my future will bring. Should I see my future as dark and dismal? Should I doubt if anything good will ever happen to me? Should I live in fear of tomorrow? No, because if I do see my future this way, then I have sealed my fate. I will have become nothing because I believe I am nothing.

I will view my life with optimism and hope for the future.

Like light and dark, good and bad, there is another view. If I see my future as light and hopeful, if I doubt anything bad will ever happen to me, and if I look forward to tomorrow with excitement, then I have also sealed my fate. I am happy because I am optimistic. I have hope for a better tomorrow. I am not worried about the failures of today because I know that things will be better tomorrow.

I will also view my life as an adventure. What happens next may be beyond my control, yet the excitement is worth the risk. I will see my life in the same way a child sees the world—with innocence and peace of heart. I will know that each day, something new and exciting will happen to me. I will know that each day, I will learn something that is important to me. Each day, I will expect that something good will happen to me. I have no fear of tomorrow because it will be better than today.

I will view my life with optimism and hope for the future.

When I look to the future with optimism, I know great things will happen to me. Life can only improve for me, and it makes me feel great enthusiasm for everything I do. There is no fear that the future will not come true, because optimism is like a star that guides me at night. As I flow through troubled waters, I simply look at the star, and I know I will arrive if I stay on course. As long as I use the star of optimism to be happy, I will always reach my goal. As I know, happiness is both the beginning and end of any goal in life. Optimism will make me happy.

I will view my life with optimism and hope for the future.

If things are bad, they will get better. If they are good, I will appreciate them more. There is always room for more optimism in my life. What will I be optimistic about? Everything. I will be optimistic about myself and have high hopes for my future. I will believe that good things will happen to me. I will be optimistic about people. I will believe they are thinking good thoughts and doing good deeds because it makes me feel better about them. I will be optimistic about my family and believe in them. My faith in them will help them overcome all odds. I will be optimistic with my enemies because I believe it will make the world a better place. I will be optimistic with the words I speak because I understand the power of words to influence others. I will be optimistic in the way I lead my life because actions and words go hand in hand. Optimism will become a way of life for me, and I will be happy as a result.

Thank you, Wakantanka, for showing me this truth.

The Fourth Cycle of the Moon

David had heard that it was important to be optimistic about life, yet he hadn't considered that it was important if he wanted to be happy. When he thought about his father and the Man, though, he knew it was true. They both looked forward to each and every day. What was it that his father always said to him?

"Tomorrow things will be better."

He didn't just say the words; he believed them. He knew that his father drew strength from the outlook—it helped him through the difficult times and allowed him to enjoy the good times. David wanted to start with this outlook right away, but he knew he had to master the ones before it. If he skipped around, he knew the outlooks would never become part of his life.

The Man began with the fourth outlook.

"People who view their life with optimism find the next outlook easy to use in their lives. Despite the fact that the next outlook is one you've heard many times, you must master it like the others before it. Setting goals helps a person stay focused on the future. Read this outlook to yourself three times a day during the fourth cycle of the moon, and it will become part of your life."

SET NEW AND INTERESTING GOALS
The Fourth Stick Needed to Fuel the Fire of Happiness

I will set new and interesting goals because I know it will make me happy.

As the sun sets in the evening, I realize that another day has gone by. Yesterday has taught me lessons, given me experiences, and has left my life forever. There is nothing I can do to get yesterday back.

Tomorrow holds great promise for me. My future is in my own hands, and there is so much to do to make it the kind of day I expect. It is the beginning of a new journey, one that will influence my life forever. Things will change tomorrow. I will act, speak, and think differently than I ever have. How will I know how to behave? How will I know where my journey takes me? The unknown can be frightening and I do not want to be afraid of tomorrow. How then can I stop this fear? I can stop it simply by setting new and interesting goals. These goals will be a map of my journey. They will allow me to lead my life with confidence. They will allow me to chart my progress toward anything I desire. They will make me think about the future.

I will set new and interesting goals.

I can control my future through my actions of today. If I want to become successful, I know there is something I can do today to help me achieve my goal. If I want to be healthier in the future, I know my goal today is to take the first step toward that goal. Daily goals are important because I know I can never reach my future goals without actions of today. I know and understand that if I do not set daily goals, I will journey through life without a map. Without a map, I will be lost, and I do not want to be lost. I want to walk with Wakantanka with confidence, and Wakantanka has given me a truth with which I lead my life. What is that truth? The truth is simple—one day there won't be a tomorrow. I will set goals today and work to achieve them, because one day I won't be able to begin them tomorrow. If I set daily goals, I will be happy.

I will also set long-term goals. Without long-term goals, my daily goals will have little effect on my life. I know that long-term goals help me face the discouragement I feel when I do not meet my daily goals. Every failure in a daily goal teaches me something. This knowledge will accumulate over time, and I will find that I have learned more from my failures than from my successes. This is why I do not fear failure or evaluate my performance on a daily basis. Just as a tree takes many years to grow strong, so must I grow strong slowly. Knowing these things helps keep me happy.

I will set new and interesting goals.

While I understand that I set goals to reach a desired end, I also know and understand that the journey toward the goal is enjoyable. What successful man is not willing to speak with pride when he tells you what he has overcome to reach his goals? What exceptional athlete is not willing to tell you with pride about the thousands of hours of work before the victory? The hard work, the successes and failures, all help people achieve their goals. I know and understand that goals are to be enjoyed while I work to achieve them, not only when I succeed. To be happy, I must set goals and understand that any failure has given me an obstacle that, once overcome, will become a source of pride for me. Goals help me feel great happiness in my heart.

I will set new and interesting goals.

I will list my goals on a daily basis. I will list both long- and short-term goals and make sure I understand what it takes to reach them. Then I will work toward achieving them. By doing so, I will be able to focus on improvement in my life. If I work to improve my life, I will be happy. Each time I reach a goal, I will quickly set another so I do not become lethargic. I understand and believe that lethargy is the seed of discontent in my life, while setting, working toward, and reaching goals makes me feel good about my future. I will be happy because the goals I set do not allow me the time to dwell on negative things in my life.

In short, I will be happy if I set new and interesting goals.

The Fifth Cycle of the Moon

David wondered what would come next. By the time he began to learn this outlook, nearly four months would have passed.

The Man began to speak about the fifth outlook.

"I wonder," he said slowly, "how you'll feel about this next outlook. I am going to ask you to do something that is very difficult. For this cycle of the moon, imagine that each day is your last on Earth, and act with this thought in your mind. This outlook, more than any other you learn, will cause others to see you in a different light. In addition, you'll see yourself in a different light. You will learn to appreciate every moment of every day and come to appreciate all life. This outlook more than any other will make you a better person. Read this outlook three times a day after you meditate during the fifth cycle of the moon."

The Man paused for a moment and then began to teach David the fifth outlook.

LIVE EACH DAY AS IF IT WERE YOUR LAST
The Fifth Stick Needed to Fuel the Fire of Happiness

I will be happy because I live this day as if it were my last.
I will not live to see tomorrow, yet I will be happy.
My life will end, yet I will be happy.
My future plans are gone forever, yet I will be happy.
It is the last day of my life, and I am happy!

There will be no more tomorrows for me. My life will end when the moon rises in the evening. I want to be sad—in my heart I feel I deserve more years. I have so much left to accomplish, so many dreams left unfulfilled. Yet, even though I want to be sad, I'm not. I am happy—more happy than I've ever been. I tell myself—I am happy! I am happy! Yet how? How can I be happy when I know there is little time left?

Because today is special, and it cannot be wasted with thoughts of sadness. *Because today I will appreciate each and every minute. There will be no time for sad thoughts! Because I*

111

know that only I control my happiness and Wakantanka *has given me the strength to feel happiness in my heart—and He wants my last day to be happy. And most of all, because I know that this day is an undeserved bonus. I have been given a day, and I know it is my last day. No one else can know when they will pass on, but I do! I know the greatest secret in the world! Knowing these things helps me feel much happiness in my heart.*

With these truths in mind, what will I do on my last day? First, I will make sure I do not waste a single moment. I will take each minute during the day and find something that makes me happy. It may be as simple as a singing bird or beautiful color, but I will notice it, appreciate it, and love it. I know that all beauty is the gift of Wakantanka *and He has given me the wisdom to appreciate it. How can I not do this for Him? He has showered the world with beauty so I can be happy. So today, on my final day, I will greet the dawn with reverence. I will find beauty in all living things. I will find beauty in nature—*

the clouds will awe me, the winds will lighten my burdens, and the seas will cleanse me of all my shortcomings. I know that today my final hours will be spent with inner peace and wonder at the beauty that surrounds me.

And yet, I will do more than notice the beauty in the world. Because it is my last day, I want to devote my full attention to it. Each minute is the single most precious thing I have, and I am happy because I know how to make the most of it. This day is my life—my entire life, and I sing with joy that I can use it as I see fit. I wake in the morning with a feeling of thanks to Wakantanka that I have this final day. I am going to make the few remaining hours the finest I have ever had in my life.

I will live each day as if it were my last.

What will I do with this last day? Why has it been given to me? There must be a reason, because so many before me have never been given this chance. It must be my last day to be happy. It must be my day to love all those close to me. It must be my day to appreciate things I never have before. These are *the things that I must do in my few precious hours that remain. I will greet each hour with excitement, and I will cherish everything because I will never see it again. I will love this last day with all my heart, and it makes me happy to know I am not wasting it with negative thoughts.*

I will live each day as if it were my last.

I am going to do things that make myself and others happy today. I will tell someone important to me how special they are in my life and will smile when I see their expression. I will help someone in need because it makes me happy to know I can do something kind today. I will make amends with my enemies because I want them to know that I value all life and want them to be happy, too. I will walk with Mother Earth and appreciate the beauty that surrounds me because I know I will laugh with wonder at the mystery of life. I will live with love and excitement in my heart because I know that tomorrow I'll be gone, and I want to be happy one last day.

And, if indeed it is true, and it is my last day, I will have lived

*my greatest day. I will have lived every minute with my fullest
zeal. I will have loved to my heart's greatest capacity. Each and
every minute will have been the happiest of my entire life.*

*And if I am wrong and it is not my last day, I will raise my
hands in victory and give thanks to* Wakantanka *for giving me
one more chance to be happy.*

The Sixth Cycle of the Moon

The thought of living each day as if it were his last seemed difficult to
David. Yet he also knew it was something he had to learn. If he could do it,
each day would hold a very special significance to him. He would appreciate
every moment and be happier because of it. This, too, was one of the things
his father probably did in his life.

The Man poured two cups of tea before he began to discuss the sixth
outlook.

"Before we learn the sixth outlook, I want you to know that every problem you face in your life will be no worse than problems others face in theirs. Problems confront each and every one of us, but the happy people are the ones who adjust to them accordingly. Think, for example, of a turtle crawling across the table. If you pound on the table with your hand, what does the turtle do? It puts his head inside his shell. This is the same thing many people do. They don't adjust to life; they retreat from it. Remember, by the time you begin to master this outlook, you will be optimistic about your life and will be setting goals. If you don't reach your goals, don't retreat; adjust to them. You will be much happier as a result. Remember, also, that to learn to do this, you must read the meaning of the outlook three times a day after meditation for the entire cycle of the moon."

He paused for a moment.

"Now, by this time, I hope you know you will have been learning for nearly six months. You'll have changed more than you'll ever know, but I'll tell you again—*master these outlooks one at a time.* Take your time and do what they say. You'll notice a wonderful change in yourself. Others will notice it, too. If you've been able to make it this far, you've been more successful than most. Please— for yourself and those who know you—do exactly as you've been told."

He cleared his throat, then began the sixth outlook.

ADJUST TO LIFE ACCORDINGLY
The Sixth Stick Needed to Fuel the Fire of Happiness

I will be happy because I adjust to life accordingly.

I know that everything I desire will not come true for me. Many times things that I desire and things that happen to me are beyond my control. It is the way of Mother Earth, it is the way it has always been, and it is the way it will always be. Why has the world been created this way? Why would Wakantanka *make such a place? Is it because He wants me to be unhappy? No, I know it is not. That is not* Wakantanka's *way.* Wakantanka *wants me to be happy and it is my duty to be happy to honor Him. Why then does it sometimes seem so difficult? Why do so many problems seem to confront me, thwarting my progress? I believe I know the answer.*

It is because I share this world with others.

I share it with nature, I share it with people, I share it with the creatures whom Wakantanka *has blessed. This is not my world; I am borrowing it from my descendants, and I am borrowing it from* Wakantanka, *I am borrowing it from all those who exist with me. And because all things share this world with others that have the same claim to its resources, I cannot control everything that happens to me. If a disease kills all the wheat in the world, there is nothing I can do to make bread. If a man owns all the cows in the world and will not share, there is nothing I can do to have beef. There are things beyond my control, yet I know and believe that* Wakantanka *had purpose when he designed the world. What, then, is this purpose? And why did He do it? These two questions have plagued man for centuries, but has an answer been found? Yes, I know the answer when I look into my heart and soul. I know His purpose.*

His purpose was to make me strong by adjusting positively to the things that happen to me in life.

What does this mean to me? It means everything! It means that I do not have to receive everything I want to be happy because I will be strong enough to adjust to life without it. It means my happiness is up to me—it depends not on what happens but instead on how I perceive and adjust to the problem. I know and believe that I can make the best out of any situation because making the best of it is completely up to me.

I am so happy now that I know that nothing will be able to get me down! If something happens, I will make something good come of it. If life gives me something unexpected, I can make a single adjustment, and something great will happen instead. I can be happy because I know this truth.

I will adjust to life accordingly.

I now know how to lead my life. I know how to be happy with each and every breath I take. It is so easy to do! I simply must adjust to anything that goes wrong with a happy attitude! I know and believe from the depths of my heart that Wakantanka *would never give me a problem so large that I cannot handle it. It is not His way. I have the strength of my forefathers in my soul to help me adjust, and I have the wisdom of* Tunkasila *to lead me to the truth. Thank you,* Wakantanka, *for giving me this knowledge and strength. I will adjust and be happy to honor You.*

I will not worry when a problem confronts me, because I will either solve the problem or adjust happily to it. I will not despair when I have lost something of value, because I know I will either find it or learn to live happily without it. I will not feel anger when others try to defeat me, because I know I will be able to be happy whether I lose or not. I will not feel lonely, because I know I will make friends if I have a happy attitude.

I will adjust to life accordingly.

I know that if I adjust to problems in my life and work to be happy despite them, I will have learned the greatest secret in the world. What can I hope to accomplish? Happiness! If I know I can adjust to problems, if I know I can be happy, then I know I can do something very few people can do. I can lead a happy life! If I am happy each and every day, then at the end of my days, I will have led a happy life. I can ask for nothing more.

I will adjust to life accordingly.

I also know that problems will come to each and every person in the world. But who are the ones who are happy despite them? The ones who adjust to problems with a happy attitude—that's who! I will also adjust to problems in the same way. I will laugh when confronted with a problem, and I will smile when things go wrong because I know I will adjust to them. I know there is nothing that can happen to me that will affect my happiness, because my view of the world comes from inside me. I will conquer life with happiness, I will live each day with joy in my heart, and I will adjust to my problems with cheer because I know it is up to me to do such things. I feel an internal strength because I know I can adjust to anything that confronts me. How horrible life would be if happiness depended on someone or something else. It would mean that only certain people would be happy. This knowledge makes me understand the wisdom of Wakantanka. I now understand why He wants me to adjust to the problems in my life. I understand why problems need not make me unhappy.

In the limited world He created, the only way He could allow all of us to be happy was to leave it up to us.

The Seventh Cycle of the Moon

David thought about the sixth outlook as he wrote it down. The way the Man had told him about *Wakantanka's* purpose made David feel good. He was glad that he alone could control his happiness by adjusting to life accordingly. He also realized that it was important to lead his life with this outlook. By doing so, he would be able to confront his problems head-on and make the best of them.

The Man began to talk about the seventh outlook.

"The next outlook teaches you the power of love. Most important, it teaches you to love yourself. If you can't love yourself, then you can't love anything. If you love yourself, you'll find that happiness takes over your life. Read the meaning of the picture three times a day after you meditate during the seventh cycle of the moon."

LEARN TO LIVE WITH, AND LOVE, YOURSELF
The Seventh Stick Needed to Fuel the Fire of Happiness

I will be happy because I know how to live with, and love, myself.

I know this is the foundation of happiness in my life. Winds can topple trees, earthquakes can stop a river from flowing, and fire can destroy a valley. The strength and power of men can destroy cities, but the power of love shall help me overcome anything that faces me. Love is the strength that binds people together. It is the most powerful thing of all. I must learn to love myself to be happy. If I don't, I will be lost in an unknown land, with despair and loneliness all around me.

I may not be attractive, I may not be intelligent, I may not say the right words or do the right things, but I know that the love of myself will open the hearts of all. If I love myself, I have an unseen strength that others will see. I will glow with happiness like the sun, and radiate love to all those who see me. I will become like Tunkasila, *and I will seem wise to all who meet me. Others will come from far away to learn from me as if I have a secret that only a few possess. I will tell them they must come to love themselves because that is the cornerstone of true wisdom and happiness.*

I will learn to live with, and love, myself.

How can I love myself? It is simple. I must look upon my life as sacred. I am special because no one else can ever be the same as me. I have abilities and thoughts that no one else has, and these make me valuable to the world. I love what I can and can't do because I know these things are unique to me. I love what I say because the words come from my soul. I love my feelings because they come from my heart. I love myself because Wakantanka *was wise and all-knowing when he created me. He makes no mistakes, and I am the most precious thing He has ever created.*

I will learn to live with, and love, myself.

I love myself for thousands of reasons. I love my words, my actions, my thoughts, and my dreams. I love myself because it makes me happy. And if I love myself and am happy, I can love all things. I can love all creatures, I can love nature, and I can love other people. Without a love of myself, these things are impossible. If I cannot love myself, I cannot love the world. If I cannot love myself, I cannot love others, because I do not feel happiness in my heart. If I cannot love myself, I cannot be happy. If I am not happy, my life is worthless.

But I know my life is not worthless! I can love! I can and do love myself because I want to be happy! I know Wakantanka created me with love, and I will love his creation. I love myself because I am meant to be happy. That is Wakantanka's greatest desire for me. From now on, I will love myself and lead my life with love in my heart. And that love will spill out of me and improve my life in every way.

I will learn to live with, and love, myself.

I will love myself because I see the world with love. I will love all creatures I see because I know each and every thing has a place in this world. I will love nature because it is beautiful and ever-changing. I will love the world because that will make it a better place.

I will learn to live with, and love, myself.

I will love myself, and I will begin to see other people with love in my heart. I will love the poor because they teach me to be charitable, I will love the rich because they teach me ambition. I will love the uneducated because they see the world in a way that I cannot. I will love the intelligent because they teach me things I would otherwise never know. I will love all people because they are special and unique, and I recognize their rarity in the world. If I see all people with love in my heart, I am happy. I will love myself and others because it makes the world a more peaceful place.

I will learn to live with, and love, myself.

I will love the things I say because I know I speak with love and goodness. I will teach that love is the power that unites all. I will teach that love can help overcome all obstacles. I will say that I love myself because I know that without these words on my lips, I cannot be happy. If I love myself, I will be able to speak these words of love. If I speak the words of love to myself and others, I will be happy. Love and happiness go hand in hand.

I will love the things I do because my way of doing things is unique. I have abilities and limitations that make the things I do unlike those of anyone before me. I love myself because I know that my actions can never be replicated. I am special, I am of immense value to the world.

I am happy because I love myself.

The Eighth Cycle of the Moon

David was glad that the Man taught him the importance of love. This was the reason he saw his father as a gentle and kind man. This was the reason his father helped those in need. His father had once told him that you don't eval-

127

uate a person on how he treats people—you evaluate him on how he treats those from whom he has nothing to gain.

The Man began to talk about the eighth outlook.

"Unhappy people place too many demands on themselves. They insist that they do everything perfectly. They allow no mistakes in their life. As you learn the next outlook, you'll understand how foolish this is. Remember to read this outlook three times a day after you meditate during the eighth cycle of the moon."

The Man began to tell David the eighth outlook he should have in his life.

Never Be a Perfectionist
The Eighth Stick Needed to Fuel the Fire of Happiness

I am happy because I never insist on perfection.

To insist on perfection is to insist on the impossible. No man, including myself, is perfect. No man has ever gone through life without a single problem or single regret. No creature is perfect. Creatures lose their lives because they cannot understand all the dangers that confront them. The world is not perfect either. Nature has caused immense destruction and loss of life. If nothing living in the womb of Mother Earth has ever experienced absolute and continual perfection, why do I insist on it for myself and others? I can experience only failure and unhappiness when I insist on perfection. Why don't I simply do my best? Why don't I ask others for their best effort? Doing my best or giving total effort is all I can ask of myself and others. I will not insist on perfection anymore. Knowing and believing in this basic truth will make me happy.

I will never be a perfectionist.

From now on, I will not insist on perfection for myself. I know perfection is an unattainable goal. If I insist on it, then I will be confronted with anger and despair—I will be unhappy. If I ask for effort instead of perfection, I will be happy. From now on, I will set goals but will not despair if they do not come out exactly as planned. I will look for the best in every effort—I will not dwell on the worst. When I work hard, I will be proud because I know I am giving my best. If my end is not achieved, I will not blame myself unless I know I did not work to my fullest potential. Because I know and understand that failure is part of human nature, I will accept failure and use it to my advantage. I will learn from failure because I know it can teach me important lessons in life. By not insisting on perfection, I find it much easier to be happy.

Because I don't expect perfection for myself, I know I can't expect perfection of others. Knowing this makes me a better person. I understand when others do not do what I ask; I sympathize when things go wrong for them; I feel their pain when they are saddened. I can only ask of them what I ask of myself— best effort. If I insist on perfection from others, I will become their enemy. If I insist on perfection, I will be cold-hearted in their eyes. If I insist on perfection, my leadership will be disregarded, because they know that perfection is unattainable. If I insist on perfection, I will never be satisfied by the performance of others. Perfection is a dream; effort is reality. I will live my life with an eye for reality—I will not live in a dream world. I will be happy because my wisdom leads me to this basic truth.

I will not insist on perfection from nature. Just as I cannot insist on perfection from myself or others, I cannot insist that nature be perfect. I will not expect the sun to shine every day, and I will not be surprised when storms create a path of ruin. I will come to expect the unexpected. I know that to insist on perfection in nature is to be the One True Power in the sky. I know I am not Wakantanka. I will not insist on perfection.

I will never be a perfectionist.

How will this affect my life and the things I do? It will make me happy. I will become more patient, more understanding, and wiser. I will be looked upon favorably by those who appreciate my kindness. I will know and understand that I cannot please everyone with the things I say and do. By not insisting on perfection, I will come to understand this important truth. By understanding this, I will find it easier to be happy.

If I insist on effort instead of perfection, I will look upon my own life with a greater understanding. I will accept, with greater patience, the problems that confront me. If I insist on effort from others rather than perfection, they will come to appreciate me as a person and friend. If I do not expect perfection, I will be happy because I see the world in a new way.

Effort, not perfection, is what I will ask of myself. Doing this will make me happy.

The Ninth Cycle of the Moon

David thought about the eighth picture. He decided he would no longer place such demands on himself.

The Man quickly moved on to the next outlook.

"Laughter is one of the keys of happiness. If a person can laugh, he can work through any problem that confronts him. It is one of the surest ways to keep yourself happy. The most beautiful thing about laughter is that it begins to make you feel better right away and is a very simple thing to do. Still, it's important to devote a cycle of the moon to learn to use it in your life. The reason is simple—most people feel uncomfortable if they laugh too much. They think others will view them as strange. Yet, it's not true. In your own life, think of the type of people you like to be around. Do you like people who laugh a lot, or those who don't? The answer is simple—and it's the same for everyone. We like to be around those who are happy—their happiness is contagious, and we feel better when we're around them."

David smiled and nodded. He knew it was true. He would read the meaning of this outlook three times a day during the ninth cycle of the moon.

The Man began.

LEARN TO LAUGH AT LIFE
The Ninth Stick Needed to Fuel the Fire of Happiness

I will be happy because I have learned to laugh at life.
Only people can laugh. No animals have this precious gift.
Animals can cry in pain, growl in fear, and feel pangs of
hunger. They can grow tired, and they can reproduce and

hunt. Many can smell and hear better than man. They do not, however, laugh. Laughter is unique to humankind. It is a gift from Wakantanka *—a gift so special He has given it to only one creature in this world. It must be very important for Him to have been so selective with this gift. From now on, I will lead my life with appreciation of this special gift.*

I will learn to laugh at life.

I will smile when problems confront me, and I will laugh when things get me down. I know that by doing these things, I will improve my life. My physical health will improve, my mental health will improve, and my emotional health will improve. Laughter will limit negative feelings in my life, laughter will make me live longer, and laughter will give me a life worth living. Knowing the power of laughter is one of the world's great secrets, and now it is mine.

I will also laugh at myself and the things I do. I will not take everything I do so seriously, because I know I am most comical when I do. Although I am the most special thing ever created, do I really believe the things I do today will have a pro-found effect on the world? Am I really that important? No, I know I'm not. What happens to me today will seem insignificant centuries from now. Why, then, should I take life so seriously? It is mine to enjoy, not to fret. Laughing at life will make me happy.

I will learn to laugh at life.

I must learn to laugh when things go wrong. I must learn to smile when there are problems. How will I do this? I must know that in time, the problems I face today will fade like a shadow as the sun sets. With laughter, I control my problems; my problems do not control me. Today, then, I will laugh more than I ever have. If I am angered, I must know that years from now, I will not remember it. If I am saddened by a friend, I must know that time will make the pain fade to distant memory. I must learn to think this way because it makes me more able to laugh and smile. If I laugh and smile, I have a power that changes my life.

What is this special power? It is simply this—laughter makes me happy. When I laugh, I become happy—no matter what is happening in my life! Why is this true? Because it is the way I am; it is the way I have been raised. When I was a child, I laughed when I was happy. When I grew older, I continued to laugh when I was happy. In time, laughter and happiness became one, and now there cannot be one without the other. If I laugh, I am happy. How do I know this is true? Because I have experienced it in my life. How many times have I been angry, and then someone made me smile, and my anger faded away? How many times have I laughed at the problems facing me because they were so overwhelming, and suddenly they seemed to be less important? It is true: To be happy, I simply must laugh.

I will learn to laugh at life.

From now on, I will laugh more often. I will wake up each morning with a smile and joyous shouts of laughter. Laughter will make all my problems seem less important. I will laugh at my failures, and they will fade to nothing; in their place will be new hope and understanding. I will laugh at my successes and realize how unimportant they are in the realm of time. Each day, I will smile and laugh because I know it makes me happy, and I truly want to be happy.

As long as I laugh, I will be happy. I will never be poor because I will feel happiness and love in my heart. I will never be uneducated because I know the greatest truth in the world. I will never be alone because happiness allows Wakantanka *to speak to my soul. I will never feel sadness because I am too busy laughing to let it take root in my life.*

I will laugh now. I will laugh again in a few minutes. I will laugh at every opportunity because it makes me happy. Wakantanka *has given me this power to help me, and I will use it. I will be happy. I will honor* Wakantanka *with happiness.*

The Tenth Cycle of the Moon

David knew that he would enjoy using this outlook. It was easy to do—in fact, it was much easier than some of the other outlooks—and it would indeed make him happy.

The Man began speaking about the final truth.

"The next outlook is the final one you need to know to be happy. It will help eliminate mistakes in your life, and it will teach you to think of another person with every act you take. Living with this outlook makes others respect you and the things you do. It will take one cycle of the moon to learn, but it is time very well spent. Do it three times a day after your meditation."

He began with the tenth and final outlook.

LEARN TO SEE THE OTHER'S POINT OF VIEW
The Tenth Stick Needed to Fuel the Fire of Happiness

I will be happy because I can see another person's point of view.

There are few things as important in the world as under-standing a loved one, a stranger, or an enemy, and seeing the world from their point of view. I become wise when I can empathize with their feelings, I realize the importance of actions or words when I see the world with their eyes; my life becomes more vibrant when I experience what they are going through. Most of all, I become kinder, gentler, and less concerned with myself. Charity begins to take root in my life, and that makes me feel good. I become happy when I help those in need. I will learn to see the other's point of view, and I will be happier as a result.

How often have I regretted an action that I took without thinking of another? How often have I felt guilt because my words hurt another? How often have I felt sadness because I caused another great pain? Too many to count. From now on, I will do no such things. I will think of others before I think of myself. I will act as Wakantanka desires—with kindness and understanding toward others.

What will I receive in return? I will receive happiness in my life. I will know I am a person who truly cares about others. I will know that I have acted with goodness in my heart. I will remove guilt, sadness, and regret from my life and replace it with dignity and love. I will find it easy to look at myself with pride and happiness when I know I have lived my life with other people in mind. I will become a symbol of hope in a world of turmoil.

I will learn to see the other's point of view.

I will also make fewer mistakes in my life if I think of another person first. I will more carefully think through the problems facing me and act in a way that makes me happy. I will take the time to learn about the concerns of those I love and take their feelings into account when I make a decision. By my acting with their concerns in mind, they will know that I truly care about them. We will grow in love, and we will grow in hope and happiness. We will have a much better life.

I will learn to see the other's point of view.

By seeing another person's point of view, I will become

more loving. I will be more patient and kind. I will not be jealous, arrogant, boastful, or rude. I will not insist on my own way or be resentful. I will bear all things, believe in the goodness of all, and my happiness will endure forever.

I will see the other's point of view.

I will be happy because I will do the right thing. I will act from concern and love, and knowing this makes me feel good about myself. I know that my charity toward others at the expense of myself is often overlooked by those around me. Yet, I do not act charitably simply for other people's good; I do it for myself. I will be happier when I do such things, because it is the way Wakantanka *wants me to act. Just as He has given of himself for us, I will give of myself to others.* Wakantanka's *way is the right way; it is a way of life that will surely make me happy.*

I will see the other person's point of view, and I will be happy.

When David was finished writing the tenth outlook, he was tired. His hand was cramped and his eyes felt a bit strained, but he didn't care. It was a small price to pay for the knowledge he had received.

David felt that these outlooks were the most important things ever written. Was there anything else in life as important as these basic truths? No, David didn't think so. These were the truths that thousands had longed to learn. These were the things that his father knew that made him so special.

David also understood why it would take almost a year to learn them. He could not simply read them once and expect them to influence his life. He had to think of them on a daily basis. It was like the Man had told him—he had to master them one at a time. If he rushed through them, they would not become part of his life. Just as it takes him many years to grow into a man, he could not change overnight.

This was going to be the best year of his life.

◎ The Lesson of the Sacred ◎ Tree, the River, and *Paha Sapa*, the Heart of Everything That Is

The Meaning of the Sixth Picture

BALANCE IN LIFE IS EXTREMELY IMPORTANT. SO FAR, YOU'VE LEARNED THE
MENTAL AND EMOTIONAL ASPECTS OF HAPPINESS. NOW IT'S TIME TO LOOK
AT THE PHYSICAL AND SPIRITUAL ASPECTS OF HAPPINESS. THESE ASPECTS
BRING YOU CLOSE TO MOTHER EARTH, AND IN RETURN, SHE LEADS YOU TO
HAPPINESS AND PEACE OF HEART.

The evening was cool and crisp, with a light easterly breeze. Tree limbs moved lazily with the wind, swaying with a hypnotic, almost spiritual motion that brought peace of heart and mind to those in tune with nature. The moon had risen high in the sky and was perched behind a thick, gray rain cloud that changed shapes as it gradually made its way across the evening sky. The moonbeams, the clouds, and the wind all worked together to create dancing shadows that leaped and flickered across the valley below. The gentle chirping of crickets and the songs of the cicadas were the only sounds that broke the silence at *Paha Sapa*. It was at times like these that you knew why these hills were sacred and were called *the heart of everything that is.*

David and the Man sat beneath the giant oak where David had learned the secret of happiness. The Man chanted softly, and his tone mixed with the sounds of nature in perfect harmony. They had not spoken for many hours. Together they had watched the sun sink below the horizon and had greeted the night with silence. In his heart, David felt peace. He looked to the stars and saw their mystery; he felt the strength of the wind on his face and heard *Wakantanka* in the creatures of the night. He was awed by this place, yet he felt as if he belonged here.

Finally, as the evening drew on, David spoke. "I have a question."

"Yes?"

"I was wondering how much everything has changed since you were a young boy."

The Man sighed and looked at the ground. He seemed almost saddened by his answer. "They have changed very much."

"How?"

"In many ways."

"Tell me, what were our people like many years ago?"

The Man thought for a long while. "We were much closer to Mother Earth in the past. Our ways have been slowly forgotten or neglected. There are too many who feel they do not have a place in the world of today."

In his heart, David knew the words were true. People do not feel a kin-ship with the world. What was it his father said? *A man's heart becomes hard when it's taken from nature. It changes him forever. It creates a lack of respect for the earth and all growing, living things, and in the end, leads to a lack of respect for humans, too.*

David felt sorrow for the Man. The world could still learn from him, but would the world ever give him the chance? It should. In the ever-changing world of today, the Man's teachings could bring stability and peace of heart to all those in need.

David questioned the Man again. "How were you taught when you were a boy?"

The Man smiled and looked at David. His dark, soft eyes brought warmth and strength to his expressions; his words were those of distant, almost forgotten memories. "When I was young, I was taught as you're being taught now—with stories, legends, and myths. When I was no older than three, I learned about the Great Spirit's circle of creation in which all is connected. It meant little when I first heard it, but in time, it taught me the sanctity of life. It taught me the need for respect, for kindness, and for patience. As I grew older, I learned to look into my heart to find the answers to the questions I had. My heart is the keeper of my spirit, and this spirit is *Wakantanka's* breath. By following my heart, I will do no wrong to those around me. Now, I learn from my visions and dreams. I learn from them because I know the time will come for me to join the spirit world. These visions and dreams are *Wakantanka's* way of guiding me."

"Were you also taught with a scroll?"

"No. I was taught with a medicine wheel. It's a symbol painted on a circular drum. There are lines in it that intersect in the middle and point in four directions. Again, it's symbolic of the circle of creation. The lines represent four aspects of ourselves—the mental, the physical, the emotional, and the spiritual. The lines also represent the gifts of the four directions. The east, where the sun rises, symbolizes beginning, joy, spontaneity, purity, birth, and trust. The south, where the sun is at its highest point, symbolizes fullness, generosity, loyalty, kindness, and a passionate involvement in the world. The west, which brings the darkness of night, teaches me spirituality. It symbolizes silence, fasting, reflection, contemplation, and humility. From the north, where the snow is white like the hair of my elders, I learned to analyze, I learned to understand and speculate. From the north, I learned to be wise."

David was intrigued. He had seen the medicine wheel in his home but had no idea what it symbolized. *Why had his father given him the scroll instead of the wheel? Could the scroll teach him the lessons of the four directions like the medicine wheel?* He asked the Man, who answered with a nod.

"In a way. You wanted to be happy—that's the purpose of the scroll. If you had wished, the scroll could have been used to teach the lessons of the medicine wheel—but that's not why you came to me. If, however, you relate the scroll and the medicine wheel, you'll find many similarities in their teachings. Think of what you've learned so far. You've learned about the mental and emotional aspects of happiness—the gifts of the north and the south. In time, the scroll will teach you the physical and spiritual aspects of happiness."

"The scroll will teach me these two aspects?" David asked in wonder.

"That, my young friend, is the meaning of the sixth picture."

Although there was only moonlight to brighten the darkness, David could see the next picture. It was a picture of a stream as it flowed through the hills. In the foreground was another tree, as there had been in the fourth picture, only this time David could not tell what kind of tree it was.

"This," the Man began, "is a very important lesson. There are three things represented in the picture."

"What are they?"

"A tree, a stream, and the hills."

"Do you know what they symbolize?"

"No," David answered quietly.

"Have you ever heard the story of the Sacred Tree?"

David shook his head.

"Then, my young friend, it's time you learn."

The Man began telling the story of the Sacred Tree.

"The Sacred Tree is the tree in this picture. It's a tree that was planted by *Wakantanka* when He created the world. People came from all around and gathered under it. There they found the miracles and wonders of *Wakantanka*. It was the most precious gift He had ever given us—it taught us how to grow with wisdom. The tree itself became one with all nature. It was related to all things—the roots of the tree grew deep into Mother Earth, and the branches reached to the Father in the Sky. The fruits of the tree were for the people. They were the lessons and gifts of *Wakantanka*—the lessons of love and compassion, generosity and patience, respect and justice, and courage and humility. The fruits were the honorable intentions of all men.

"The life of the tree is the life of us all when we are one with *Wakantanka*. If people leave the shadow of the tree, they forget the lessons of *Wakantanka*. They become evil as they turn from the tree. They forget the honorable intentions *Wakantanka* wants to find in all of us. They become filled with sorrow and despair. They argue with each other; and they lie, cheat, and steal to get what they want. They lose their dreams and visions, and they forget how to live. They are filled with sadness. Little by little, everything they touch is destroyed.

149

"It was foretold that these things would happen. The people would leave the shade and forget all they had learned. *Wakantanka* would not let the tree die, though, because if he did, then the people would die. As long as the tree lives, the people live. Yet *Wakantanka* also knew that the people would one day return to the shadow of the tree and begin once again to take of its fruit.

"Where is this tree, you wonder? It's in each and every one of us. Yet, many can't find it. They are filled with despair, and despair blocks them on their journey. In order to find this tree, in order to be happy again, you must learn from *Wakantanka*."

The Man paused for a long while.

"You cannot learn about *Wakantanka* through books. They are not enough. Instead, turn to the whole of His creation—turn to Mother Earth. You will learn as much there as you would from anything you read. Understand that if you take the books and place them in nature, then the sun, the wind, the rain, and the creatures will destroy them in time. Then you can learn nothing from them. Yet, Mother Earth is never destroyed. She will teach all you need to know.

"All living creatures depend on *Wakantanka,* for it is He who created the sun, the wind, the water, and the earth. When I was young, I couldn't help but look around me and know that some great power created this. Because

Wakantanka created us all, I must honor all He created. I must act with kindness and love to all others, and think lastly of myself. In return, *Wakantanka* will give me inner peace.

"Now, I find that I feel closest to Mother Earth when I sit directly on the ground with nothing to separate the soil from my body. I'm in tune with Her, and I can think more deeply. In my life, I really have a single duty—and that is the daily recognition of *Wakantanka*. It's more important to me than food or water. Each morning at daybreak, I go to the river, take my moccasins off, and step to the river's edge. I then throw handfuls of water on my face and my body. After the bath, I stand and face the dawn and offer my own prayer—and I make sure I do these things alone. Each soul must meet the morning sun, the new earth, and *Wakantanka* alone. During the day when I come across something that is beautiful—a waterfall, a rainbow, or a dew-filled meadow—I pause for an instant in an attitude of love and worship for *Wakantanka*. By doing this, I feel a closeness with *Wakantanka*. I feel love in my heart. I feel a happiness that transcends all I do. This is *Wakantanka's* precious gift—He gives me happiness when I honor Him."

The Man paused again. "Take the time each day to find something beautiful. Each morning, thank *Wakantanka* for the world he created, feel His beauty within you, see beauty all around you, and in return, He shall give you peace of heart. He shall give you happiness."

David knew he had felt the lack of *Wakantanka* in his life in the days after his sister had died. The emptiness in his heart had caused him to cry so often that his eyes had swelled. Yet, had *Wakantanka* really left him at this time? Or . . . were his cries actually prayers for guidance, and hadn't they been answered? David knew he had not simply found the Man, but had been guided to him. He had been led by his father, his sister . . . and *Wakantanka*.

The Man looked at the scroll while David thought quietly. When David was ready, he turned to the next symbol—the river.

"The river," the Man began, "can speak to anyone who listens to it. It teaches us the meaning of life. It laughs, it cries, it moves, and it is continually connected—as is all life. The river is the power of our people; it brings water to our crops and cleanses our bodies. We use it to cook and live. As with fire, we use it to improve our lives and make them easier. Yet, unlike fire, without it we die."

"The river, my young friend, is symbolic of the physical aspect of ourselves. The river moves, and so do we when we exercise. The river cleanses, and so does physical activity. The river teaches us the meaning of life; physical activity gives us the chance to be alone and learn about ourselves. A person cannot be whole unless there is balance in life. To be happy, this aspect of life can't be ignored."

David looked confused. "Do you mean I have to exercise to be happy?"

"Yes. The physical aspect of oneself is an aspect that is neglected more than any other. Yet, if neglected, there is no balance in life. I don't want you to think that you must exercise vigorously, *but you must exercise regularly and do not indulge in overeating or drinking.* The river is necessary for us to live—you will die without physical activity or if you do not care what you place in your body. Perhaps you won't die physically, but the lack of balance will eventually ruin some of your greatest pleasures in life. Happiness is just as dependent on this aspect as it is on the others. The dependence is simply different."

"Why is it so important?"

"Because it cleanses your soul and gives you the chance to think and dream. It increases your strength, stamina, and love of life. It brings you closer to Mother Earth and gives you the balance you need in life. It can be as simple as a walk or a swim. Mother Earth will welcome you in any way you choose to be with Her. *Take the time to exercise daily, and eat and drink in moderation. In time you will come to know yourself, and your life will have balance. You will find happiness as a result."*

David looked at the picture of the river. For many minutes, he was lost in thought. He knew it was true—just as his forefathers, the Lakota Warriors, had to be healthy, so must he.

When he was ready, he asked the Man the meaning of the third symbol. "What do the hills in this picture mean?"

"It means, my friend, that you have almost learned everything you need to know. The hills in the picture are the hills you are in today. They are *Paha Sapa,* the heart of everything that is. They are sacred and holy. They are the center of understanding. As you swim in the river, past the Sacred Tree, with the lessons of the scroll in your mind, you will arrive at *Paha Sapa*. You will have the answers you looked for; there will be nothing more for you to learn. You will have become a man from the North—you will have become wise."

"But I'm so young."

"Wisdom has nothing to do with age. Wisdom is truth that comes from looking to your heart for your answers and thinking of others before yourself. Wisdom gives you life. It gives you knowledge. It gives you peace of heart and soul. It shows that life is nothing but the flash of lightning in the distance, the smoky breath of the buffalo in winter, and the drops of dew that vanish with the sunrise. Life and happiness, my young friend, are as beautiful as anything *Wakantanka* has ever created."

The Man wrote the meaning of the sixth picture on the new scroll.

THE PHYSICAL AND SPIRITUAL ASPECTS OF HAPPINESS

❀ *The spiritual and physical aspects of happiness are just as important as the mental and emotional aspects of happiness.*

❀ *Rise each day with love in your heart, take the time to look for something beautiful, find peace in the mystery of creation, and give thanks to* Wakantanka *for creating the beautiful world in which we live. You'll find happiness in everything you do.*

❀ *Come to know yourself through physical activity. Feel healthier, live longer, dream, and cleanse yourself with regular exercise, and you'll find balance in your life. You'll be happier as a result.*

⚬⚬ The Lesson of the Seasons ⚬⚬
The Meaning of the Seventh Picture

CHANGE IS SOMETIMES NECESSARY. AVOID THINGS THAT BOTHER YOU IF YOU CAN, AND CHANGE THE THINGS THAT UPSET YOU. IF YOU'RE UNHAPPY, TAKE THE TIME TO THINK OF WHAT WOULD MAKE YOU HAPPY, AND MAKE THE NECESSARY CHANGES. YOUR LIFE WILL BE IMPROVED AS A RESULT.

David looked at the scroll. There was a medicine wheel, divided into four parts, with four pictures showing the change of seasons. Snow covered the branches in one part, the trees began to bud in another, the leaves were a full green in the next, and the leaves littered the ground in the final picture.

"The final picture," the Man said, "is very simple to explain. We can do it now or we can wait until tomorrow."

"I'd like to learn it now if I could. I'm sure my father is worried about me. I think I'll be leaving early tomorrow morning."

"As you wish, David. Each of us must make our decisions. This picture, in fact, is also about decisions."

"It is?"

"Yes. Do you see the change in seasons? They are representative of change in your life. All creation, including yourself, is in a state of constant change. There are two kinds of change in the world: the coming together of things, and the coming apart of things. Both are necessary and are connected. Sometimes it's difficult to see how they're connected, but usually that's due to our standpoint—the place from where we view the change. Our standpoint can inhibit our ability to think clearly."

"How does this relate to happiness?"

"It relates in a number of ways. You've learned so much about happiness—and you've learned that it comes from within you. Yet, there are times when your life will never be in balance unless you change something. Sometimes, things in your life must change—they must come apart."

"Why?"

"Because there are very few people who can really master themselves. I can be happy in any situation, but many can't. While each of us should try to learn to control our emotions, some may never succeed. For this reason, the scroll teaches us its final lesson. *If there is something that makes you unhappy in your life, change it if you can.* If it's a small change, you'll find it's easy to make. If it's a major change, take the time to analyze your situation. If you believe you'll be better off after the change, make it. Our people, for example, had difficult choices—to fight the armies or go to the reservation. We could live in poverty with little freedom, or die. We chose the reservations because they were the lesser of two evils. Our way of life had been taken from us, yet we lived. To our people, life is precious. We changed our ways, and though some of us could never adapt, many have. We are still a culture; our ancient lessons still find their way into the lives of our young people. Yes, change can be difficult, but if your situation calls for it, answer the call. *Wakantanka* gave you strength for many reasons—and one of His reasons was for you to change the things that make you unhappy."

The Man wrote the final lesson on the new scroll.

CHANGE

❀ *You must make many decisions in your life. These decisions sometimes call for change.*

❀ *If there is something in your life that makes you unhappy, you may have to change it.*

❀ *Change can sometimes be difficult, but do not be afraid. If you follow your heart and think of others, the change will improve your life.*

❀ *Take the time to think of what makes you unhappy, find what would make you happy, and make the change. It will make you happier in the end.*

✇ The Lesson of the Journey ✇

DAVID WENT ON THE JOURNEY TO LEARN HOW TO BE HAPPY. IN THE PROCESS, HE ALSO LEARNED A LITTLE BIT ABOUT HIMSELF. I HOPE YOU TOO HAVE LEARNED. IT'S UP TO YOU, MY FRIEND, TO MAKE YOURSELF HAPPY.

The two sat in silence for a long while. David knew his lesson had ended. He bowed his head and smiled to himself. He was overwhelmed by a feeling of peace and inner strength, and tears began to well in his eyes.

They weren't tears of sadness, but tears of thanks, for he knew he had been given a gift more valuable than anything else he would ever receive again. Although he was still a young boy, he knew that in his heart and soul, he was much older than he had been a few days ago.

Happiness . . .

The gift of happiness would live forever in his heart and in the hearts of all who know the truth. When he had arrived at *Paha Sapa,* he had been tired. He had been weakened, and his spirit had left him. He no longer cared about himself. Yet now he was strong again. The blood surged through his veins, his heart pounded strongly in his chest, and he could stand with pride and face the dawn with dignity and respect. As long as the sun shines and the rivers flow, David knew he would be happy.

What had he really learned? He had learned the meaning of life itself. He knew that to sit on the ground and meditate about life and its meaning, that to accept the kinship of all creatures, that to understand how his feelings and actions are interconnected, that to know he can be happy with the lessons of the scroll in mind, was to infuse into his being the true essence of *Wakantanka's* wisdom.

How much had people lost when they stopped doing these things?

They had lost everything. They had lost their great teacher—their inner self—when they left the land and put faith in others to show them the truth.

Yet now, he felt he was part of nature again. He was *Wakantanka's* special child. *Wakantanka* had led him to safety. *Wakantanka* had led him to *Tunkasila.*

He had been led to wisdom.

Tunkasila was more than simply a man. Much, much more. He knew the lessons of Mother Earth. He was spiritual, wise, and filled with peace. He was a person who could communicate with his inner soul and teach others to do the same.

Most important, he knew how to teach lessons in such a way as to make it impossible to ever forget them. David had learned with stories, visions, legends, and a journey. He had listened and had been heard. He understood that his journey to see the Man was necessary in order to learn the truth. He knew he would not have believed in the teachings of the scroll unless he had left his family and gone to *Paha Sapa*.

David looked at the two scrolls. He picked up the painted one and handed it to the Man. He put the new scroll, with the meanings written on it, in his pocket.

"I want you to have this as a gift. I know my father would have wanted you to keep it. Thank you for all you've done."

The Man bowed his head graciously but did not reply.

David sensed there was little more to say. Instead, David looked at the *wicahpis* as his father had done when he first handed the scroll to him. They were beautiful, powerful, and mysterious.

They were like *Tunkasila*.

Early the next morning, David left *Paha Sapa*. *Tunkasila* was nowhere to be found. David looked for him for nearly an hour, but in the end decided that *Tunkasila* must have wanted to be alone. Strangely, he felt no regret even though they didn't say good-bye. He felt that the two of them had developed a bond that couldn't be broken by his leaving *Paha Sapa*. They would always be connected, both in nature and in their souls. The visions, the lessons—they would stay with David always. Just as he would carry his sister in his heart, he would carry the Man there, also.

The journey home was much shorter than David had expected. Just an hour after leaving, David was able to catch a ride that took him to within a few miles of home. He sat in the back of a pickup truck, with two dogs, and felt the wind blow against his skin and the sun shine on his face. The sights and sounds were wonderful—an old dirt road surrounded by valleys and meadows, birds flying overhead, the roar of the engine—everything felt as it should.

After getting off the truck, David walked to the cemetery where his sister was buried. Just as he had hoped, his father had kept the headstone clear while he was away. David bent down and felt the earth that now surrounded his sister. He took a scoop of dirt, looked at it, then let it fall through his fingers. He thought quietly for many minutes. *She is forever at peace,* he knew, *and her visions with him would come less often.* David knew he could honor her memory with happiness. Her spirit was now free of any Earthly worries.

David wiped the sweat from his forehead. It was going to be hot later in the afternoon. The sun was already scorching. David sighed as he looked at his sister's grave again.

"Thank you," he whispered.

The wind howled in reply.

As he began to leave the cemetery, David suddenly felt dizzy. His mouth went slightly dry, and his breathing quickened. His heart raced and he lost his balance. He fell and stood up shakily. Then he fell again. He fainted.

The next thing David remembered was awakening. As he dreamed, he felt someone shake him. David's eyes wearily opened. As he lay on the ground, he looked up and saw his father standing over him with a concerned look on his face.

"Are you all right?" his father asked.

"I . . . I guess so," David stuttered. He cleared his throat.

"What happened?"

"I don't know. I just got dizzy all of a sudden."

His father sighed in relief.

"Let me help you up," he said as he offered his hand.

David took it and stood. His legs were still a bit shaky. He dusted off his clothing. "I was on my way home to talk to you. You wouldn't believe what's happened to me."

The father smiled. "You found the meaning of the scroll, didn't you?"

David nodded quickly. "Uh-huh. Actually, I had a bit of help from the Man in the Hills. I couldn't have done it without him."

His father raised his eyebrows in surprise. "You spoke to *Tunkasila?*"

"Yes," David said as he nodded. "I was at his cabin for many days. He's a great teacher."

The father smiled again.

David looked at him curiously and asked, "Why are you smiling?"

"My son, I'm proud you've learned the scroll. Very few can ever find the truth. You're a very special young man. *Tunkasila* enters the minds of only those who can understand."

"What do you mean?"

"David," he said as he took his son by the shoulder, "you say you were gone for many days?"

"Yes," he replied cautiously.

"But how could that be? *I gave you the scroll only last night.* You had a dream. I saw you leave the house last night and walk to the cemetery. I followed close behind you and stayed with you all night."

"That's impossible. . . . "

"No. It's the truth."

"But I saw him! He even gave me a new scroll. I have it here in my pocket. . . . "

David reached for the scroll and removed it. He unrolled it carefully.

It was the same scroll his father had given him. The one he thought he had given *Tunkasila*. He looked at his father with wide eyes. "You mean it was a dream?"

His father shrugged. "Who is to say what is dream and what is reality?"

"But . . . but I talked to him."

"And I'm sure he spoke to you. As I said, *Tunkasila* visits few minds that can understand him."

David looked around the cemetery and felt a surge of warmth flow into him. A dream? A *vision*? He had never left the house, but he had learned the meaning of the scroll?

But that's impossible! I did go on a journey. . . . I found the lessons of Iktumi and learned the story of the Sacred Tree. I learned the ten outlooks and found the meaning of meditation and prayer! I couldn't have learned it all in one night . . . especially if I was still asleep!

His father, who seemed to have read his mind, said softly, "Dreams can be very real, David. Who is to say where they come from? Perhaps *Wakantanka* inspired your dream. He is capable of anything. Perhaps you did go on a journey, but if you did, my son, *you did not do it in this world*. I gave you the scroll last evening, and you came here. I finally awakened you when I heard you begin to moan. Your dream was fading, and your soul was struggling to enter this world once again."

"But how?"

"You desired the truth, my son. You found the answer you had been searching for."

David furrowed his brow. His father put his arm around him and started out of the cemetery.

"Let's go back to the house. You must be very hungry. Every journey, even those by a soul, makes a person hungry."

As they walked back to the house, David looked over his shoulder to the Black Hills far in the distance. For a moment, he thought he could see the cabin and the billowing plume of smoke from the fireplace. . . .

But of course, it wasn't there.

Or was it?

∞ Afterword ∞

This book is intended to help those individuals who want to learn about themselves and improve their outlook on life. *In no way is it intended to be used as a cure for clinical depression.*

Depression is one of the least understood and improperly diagnosed disorders in America today. Estimates indicate that up to 25 percent of all Americans suffer from clinical depression at least once in their lives. Most forms of depression can be successfully treated by a competent professional. Phrases such as "snap out of it" or "it can't be that bad" do nothing to help the person in need. The problem is physical, not mental.

If you or someone you know is suffering from severe depression, please get medical help. It will make a world of difference.

◈◈ A Note to My Readers ◈◈

David's character is a composite of many Native Americans I've met over the years. His family is also typical of those one can find on reservations around the country, including my own. When I was young, my sister died of tuberculosis, my mother died when I was seven, and my father passed away five years later when I was twelve. After their deaths, my brothers and sisters raised me until I left the reservation to attend Haskell Institute, an Indian boarding school in Lawrence, Kansas.

Reservations have changed little since I was a child. Even today, I have a hard time counting the Lakota blessings while so many are hungry and homeless on the reservation. Adults very seldom reach their seventies, and every year, a little more of the tradition of the Indian ways is forgotten.

In my work as National Spokesperson for Running Strong for American Indian Youth®, we help American Indian people meet their immediate survival needs while implementing and supporting programs designed to create opportunities for self-sufficiency and self-esteem. Running Strong drills water wells to bring fresh water, supports organic gardening programs and constructs tribal food banks to fight hunger, supports medical clinics to provide kidney dialysis to those in need, and repairs and builds new homes as a solution to the housing crisis. We also support athletic and cultural programs for tribal youth. All of our programs are designed and implemented by local Indian people.

Progress has been good. In close to fifteen years, Running Strong has completed over 278 wells on the Pine Ridge Indian Reservation in South Dakota, constructed two Indian-owned and operated kidney dialysis clinics, built a Head Start Center on the Rosebud Indian Reservation, and built a youth center on the Cheyenne River Indian Reservation. In addition, Running Strong annually supports over 260 individual and community gardens on the Pine Ridge Indian Reservation. We have also repaired over a hundred homes, donated thousands of pounds of food, and supported numerous cultural programs/camps for tribal youth throughout Indian country. Since its inception, Running Strong has donated millions of dollars in cash grants, goods, and services to American Indians.

I am very proud of the work Running Strong is doing for Native Americans. I want to thank everyone who has made these programs possible—ranging from individuals who have given their time and expertise to national organizations to philanthropists who have provided essential, substantial financial support. If you would like more information on Running Strong for American Indian Youth®, please write to me at the following address:

Billy Mills
Running Strong for American Indian Youth
8815 Telegraph Road
Lorton, VA 22079
E-mail**: info@indianyouth.org**
Please visit our website at: **www.indianyouth.org**

⦿ About Billy Mills ⦿

Billy Mills was raised on the Pine Ridge Indian Reservation in South Dakota. After breaking numerous high school track records, he received an athletic scholarship to the University of Kansas, where he received a B.S. in physical education. Upon graduation, he was commissioned as an officer in the United States Marine Corps. After training for only eighteen months, in only the sixth 10,000-meter run of his life, Billy stunned the world in what has been called the greatest upset in Olympic history when he won the gold medal at the 1964 Tokyo Olympics.

Billy's story was dramatic enough to make into a movie in 1983. *Running Brave* starred Robby Benson and was produced by Englander Productions. For many years, Billy has been one of the most successful and inspirational speakers in America, drawing packed crowds across the country.

Billy has served on the President's Council on Physical Fitness and Sports, was named one of the Ten Outstanding Young Americans by the Jaycees in 1972, and was selected as a 1990 Healthy American Fitness Leader.

He is a member of numerous halls of fame, including the United States Olympic Hall of Fame, the United States Track and Field Hall of Fame, the Kansas Hall of Fame, the San Diego Hall of Fame, and the National High School Hall of Fame.

More important, Billy hasn't forgotten his heritage. He is national chairman of Running Strong for American Indian Youth, a project of Christian Relief Services. Together, Billy and Running Strong work to improve the quality of life on reservations around the United States.

About Nicholas Sparks

Nicholas Sparks is the author of the *New York Times* bestsellers *The Notebook* and *Message in a Bottle*. Nicholas lives in North Carolina with his wife and two sons.

We hope you enjoyed this Hay House book.
If you would like to receive a free catalog featuring additional
Hay House books and products, or if you would like
information about the Hay Foundation, please contact:

Hay House, Inc.
P.O. Box 5100
Carlsbad, CA 92018-5100

(760) 431-7695 or **(800) 654-5126**
(760) 431-6948 (fax) or **(800) 650-5115 (fax)**

Please visit the Hay House Website at: **www.hayhouse.com**